THE UNITED STATES PRESIDENTS

DWIGHT D.
EISENHOWER
OUR 34TH PRESIDENT

by Sarah Hansen

The Child's World®
childsworld.com

1980 Lookout Drive • Mankato, MN 56003-1705
800-599-READ • www.childsworld.com

ACKNOWLEDGMENTS
Content Adviser: Carol Hegeman, Supervisory Historian,
Eisenhower National Historic Site, Gettysburg, Pennsylvania

PHOTOS
Cover and page 3: World History Archive/Newscom (detail)
Interior: Agence Quebec Presse/Newscom, 12; Associated Press,
15, 29, 31, 34, 36, 39 (right); Bettmann via Getty Images, 30;
Dwight D. Eisenhower Presidential Library & Museum, 5, 11, 35, 38
(bottom left); Everett Collection/Newscom, 21, 23, 24, 26, 32; Everett
Historical/Shutterstock.com, 20; Franklin D. Roosevelt Presidential
Library & Museum, 16; J. R. Eyerman/The LIFE Picture Collection via
Getty Images, 28; Paul Schutzer/The LIFE Picture Collection via Getty
Images, 37; Underwood Archives/UIG/Bridgeman Images, 19; US
National Archives and Records Administration, 6, 7, 9, 13, 18, 38 (top
left), 39 (left); World History Archive/Newscom, 4 and 38 (right)

ISBN 9781503844254 (REINFORCED LIBRARY BINDING)
ISBN 9781503846906 (PORTABLE DOCUMENT FORMAT)
ISBN 9781503848092 (ONLINE MULTI-USER EBOOK)
LCCN 2019957694

Printed in the United States of America

CONTENTS

*Dwight D. Eisenhower,
who served as president
from 1953 to 1961,
was an extremely
popular president.*

CHAPTER ONE

A MILITARY PATH

Dwight David Eisenhower, one of the greatest generals of the 20th century, waged his first war before he was five years old. The enemy was a hissing goose in his uncle's farmyard. Time after time the large, bad-tempered fowl chased the boy back into the house. Finally Dwight's uncle made him a weapon—a broomstick with most of the straw cut off. With this Dwight became the new boss of the back yard.

Eisenhower later wrote that he learned an important lesson from those first battles—to always have an advantage when dealing with an enemy. He would fight other battles and learn many more lessons throughout his life. These experiences prepared him for his greatest accomplishments as a victorious general in World War II and as the 34th president of the United States.

Dwight was born in Denison, Texas, on October 14, 1890. He was the third of David and Ida Eisenhower's seven sons. When he was almost two years old, the family moved to Abilene, Kansas.

Before he became president, Dwight D. Eisenhower was a celebrated World War II general.

Dwight had a happy childhood and later wrote, "If we were poor, we were unaware of it . . . we were a cheerful and vital family." He was aware, however, of the rivalry between the boys on the south side of town (where he lived), and the boys on the north side (where the richer

Dwight's family did not have much money, but they were happy, hardworking, and honest. They lived in a small, simple home made of clapboard. Dwight (center) later remembered that his childhood home had less floor space than his office at the Pentagon, the US military headquarters in Washington, DC.

families lived). Sometimes the north-side boys teased Dwight about his tattered clothing or hand-me-down shoes. He often got into fights, and was known as a good fighter with an angry temper. Dwight's mother did not approve of his fighting, however. Ida Eisenhower was a pacifist, a person who believes in peace. She encouraged her son to find other ways to solve his problems.

As a boy, Dwight (center) lived in a small town. He enjoyed all the benefits that life in the country could provide. He spent time outdoors, fishing and hunting in the nearby wilderness. He also enjoyed going camping with his friends. He is shown here on a 1907 camping trip.

In high school, Dwight turned his competitive spirit to sports. During his senior year, he became a star football player. His favorite subject at school was American history. "Since those early years," he later said, "history of all kinds, and certainly political and military, has always intrigued me."

At one time or another, all of Dwight's brothers had the nickname "Ike." At school, Edgar was known as "Big Ike" and Dwight was known as "Little Ike." Dwight turned out to be the one who kept the nickname throughout his life.

When he graduated from high school, Ike, as he was called, couldn't afford the **tuition** for college. After working for two years, he was admitted to the United States Military Academy at West Point, New York, where the government would pay for his college education. Ike was thrilled at this opportunity, but it was difficult for his mother to see him go. She knew he would become a soldier, and she hated to think of him going to war. Ike's youngest brother told him how she had wept after he left for West Point. Ike knew that his mother was worried about his future.

"She was very religious," he remembered later. "She believed that violence was wicked and wrong." Although Ike would be a soldier for much of his life, his mother's beliefs would always have a strong influence on him. He believed that the nation should strive for peace whenever possible.

Team sports were important at West Point. They taught cooperation and teamwork, and these were good qualities for soldiers to have. Football was Ike's main interest, and he was an outstanding player. He was terribly disappointed when injuries ended his football career, but he went on to graduate with the class of 1915.

Ike loved sports. He played both football and baseball at Abilene High School. He played football at West Point (left) during his second year there. After a knee injury forced him to quit playing, he assisted the team's coaching staff.

Ike's first assignment was at Fort Sam Houston, Texas. There he met Mamie Geneva Doud, the daughter of a wealthy family from Denver, Colorado. Ike and Mamie began seeing a lot of each other, and soon fell in love. Since Mamie loved parties and pretty clothes, some of her friends thought Ike was too poor for her. But Mamie didn't care. She and Ike were married on July 1, 1916.

Soon after that, the United States was at war. Germany and the Austro-Hungarian Empire had been fighting with other European countries for several years in what later became known as World War I. The Germans were using their submarines to sink ships from other nations, including the United States. In 1917, President Woodrow Wilson asked the US Congress to declare war on Germany, marking the beginning of America's role in World War I.

Ike immediately wrote to the War Department and asked to be sent to Europe to fight in the war. He was disappointed when he was ordered to Camp Colt, near Gettysburg, Pennsylvania. His job was to train soldiers to use a new weapon, the tank. He did his job so well that he later received a medal. He would apply to join the action overseas many times during the war, but each time the War Department refused. It said he was needed to train soldiers at home.

When the war was over, Ike was transferred to Camp Meade, Maryland. There he met General Fox Conner, who was to have a major influence on his career. Ike was assigned to be a staff officer under Conner's command in Panama, where the army was guarding the **Panama Canal.**

Ike and Mamie went to Panama early in 1922. The tropical climate was hot and humid. Their house was infested with bats and the roof leaked. But Ike later wrote that this tour of duty was one of the most interesting and important tours of his life because of his commanding officer, General Fox Conner.

Ike told Conner that he was no longer interested in military history because the history classes at West Point had been so dull. Conner set out to change Ike's mind. First, he gave him historical novels to read. These were invented stories set in real times of war. He also loaned Ike books on the military history of the same time periods described in the novels. Soon Ike was fascinated. He and Conner had deep discussions about the military decisions described in these books.

Eisenhower had the use of General Conner's large library for the three years he spent in Panama. He read and discussed dozens of books. General Conner purposely exposed Eisenhower to all these materials. He was convinced that there would soon be another war, and he thought Eisenhower should be prepared.

With the help of General Conner, Eisenhower was admitted to the Command and General Staff School at Fort Leavenworth, Kansas. All of the other students had been to another school in preparation for this one. Eisenhower was worried that he would not be able to compete with them, but he found that his work with General Conner had prepared him very well. He graduated at the top of his class of 245 students. Ike also graduated at the head of his class from the Army War College in Washington, DC.

In 1928, Ike was sent to France. His job was to write a guide to World War I battlefields and to study the terrain, railroads, and highways of France. He didn't know how useful this information would be to him later, when he led the invasion of France in World War II.

In 1933, Ike became an aide to General Douglas MacArthur, the US Army's chief of staff. Two years later, he went with MacArthur to work in the Philippines. By the end of the 1930s, it was clear that General Conner's prediction of another global war was coming true. In 1939, Ike left MacArthur to become involved in the war preparations. He had missed the chance to fight in World War I, but in the years after, his military path had prepared him to play a major role in World War II.

To study for his classes at Fort Leavenworth, Ike and a friend created a "war room." They converted a room in his house into an imitation of a command center where generals meet to make decisions about battles. They had maps all over the walls, a large table in the center of the room, and many shelves full of reference books.

FAMILY LIFE

After Ike and Mamie were married in 1916, they lived in a small apartment at Fort Sam Houston. Ike and Mamie liked to have friends over for dinner and to play cards. In fact, they had so many parties, their friends called their home "Club Eisenhower."

Their first child, Doud Dwight, was born in September of 1917. The family lived together at Camp Meade, Maryland, where the baby became a favorite of the soldiers in Ike's unit. They had a little uniform made for him and sometimes took him on drills. When Doud died in early 1921 of a serious illness called scarlet fever, it was the greatest tragedy of Ike's life. Little Doud was just over three years old.

The Eisenhowers' second son, John Sheldon Doud Eisenhower, was born in August of 1922. As John grew older, he enjoyed talking to his father and going with him to work. They also played tennis together, and John usually won. Ike was delighted when John decided to attend West Point and pursue a career in the army. Dwight (center), Mamie, and John are pictured above in 1933 in Washington, DC.

Ike's frequent moves throughout his military career kept him away from his family much of the time, but he was happiest when they were all together.

CHAPTER TWO

A GREAT GENERAL

When Eisenhower returned home to the United States, World War II had already begun. The origins of World War II could be traced to the end of World War I. After Germany's defeat in World War I, its leaders were forced to sign the **Treaty** of Versailles. This treaty stated that the war was entirely Germany's fault. It punished Germany by taking away much of its farmland and livestock, one-tenth of its factories, and all of its colonies. The German navy was abolished and its army was drastically reduced. In the years that followed, the German people struggled with poverty and food shortages.

When the **Nazi Party** came to power in the early 1930s, Germans still faced these hardships. The Nazi Party gave them someone to blame and hope for a better life. The Nazis blamed other countries for the difficulties that Germany faced. They also blamed the Jewish people, who they claimed were destroying Germany. The Nazis promised to make things better, even if it meant another war—and the violent removal of all Jews from Europe.

Eisenhower understood the cost of war. "I hate war as only a soldier who has lived it can, only as one who has seen its brutality."

In 1940 and 1941, the Nazis conducted bombing raids against England, in what became called the Blitz. Shown here are children sitting outside the ruins of their home in the suburbs of London in 1940.

World War II began in Europe in 1939 when Germany invaded Poland. In response, England and France declared war on Germany. By 1940, the Germans had already invaded Poland, Holland, Belgium, Luxembourg, and most of France. The Nazis were bombing London every day. The British were fighting desperately to hold out against them, but the Germans were winning the war.

The United States was not involved yet, but it seemed clear that it would not be able to stay out of the war forever. Back in the United States, Eisenhower helped with the preparations for the time when Americans would be called to serve. His first assignment was to train soldiers and practice war **maneuvers** in Fort Lewis, Washington. Then he was sent to Louisiana to participate in war games, in which 400,000 troops practiced for the real war. Eisenhower became well known for his winning **strategies,** and he earned a promotion to brigadier general.

Even as the military was planning strategies and soldiers were practicing for battles, public opinion in the United States was still divided. Most people hoped the **Allies,** as the countries fighting the Germans were called, would win. Some thought America should help the Allies, while other people were **isolationists** and felt that America should stay out of the war no matter what.

Fewer Americans paid attention to what was happening on the other side of the world. Japan was attacking Asian countries. It had invaded China in 1937. By 1939, it was trying to gain more territory in East Asia. People in the United States paid little attention to the problems there until December 7, 1941.

On that day, Japan attacked Pearl Harbor, a US military base in Hawaii. Thousands of Americans were killed and injured, and several US battleships were destroyed. The next day, the United States declared war on Japan. All across America thousands of young men immediately lined up to join the armed forces and fight for their country. Japan's allies, Germany and Italy, then declared war on the United States on December 11, 1941.

General Eisenhower was not a formal man. He once said that when the soldiers called him Ike, "I knew everything was going well."

Within a week of the attack, the US Army chief of staff, General George G. Marshall, ordered Eisenhower to report to Washington. There he would help with war strategy. Marshall was so impressed with Eisenhower, he **promoted** him to major general.

On December 7, 1941, Japan bombed Pearl Harbor in Hawaii. This act killed 2,403 Americans and wounded more than a thousand. The next day, the United States declared war. In this photo, young men in New York line up outside a US Army recruitment office, eager to enlist following the attack on Pearl Harbor.

In 1942, Eisenhower was appointed commander of all the American troops in Europe, with the rank of lieutenant general.

German victories were mounting. German forces had conquered most of Europe and were gaining vast areas of Russian territory. In the south, German tank units were moving across North Africa.

The Allies decided to invade North Africa first. Eisenhower's head-quarters were under the Rock of Gibraltar at the western end of the Mediterranean Sea. From there, he directed the landing of Allied troops on North African beaches in November of 1942. By 1943, they had taken much of North Africa from the Nazis.

The German general Eisenhower fought against in North Africa was known as The Desert Fox. His real name was Erwin Rommel. He was well respected for his military skill and personal bravery by both the Germans and his Allied enemies. He once called the fighting in North Africa "the war without hate."

Eisenhower ordered his troops back onto the ships. They sailed across the Mediterranean and quickly conquered the Italian island of Sicily, which is off the country's southern coast. Allied forces then invaded Italy's mainland. The Italian government surrendered almost immediately.

Finally, the Allied forces were winning battles. Eisenhower was rewarded with a promotion to four-star general, the second highest rank in the army. He was put in charge of the biggest Allied attack of all, the invasion of **occupied** France.

Eisenhower knew it was important that soldiers from all the Allied countries see themselves as part of a single fighting force. He worked with British, French, and other Allied leaders to plan the enormous attack, called "Operation Overlord." The secret date of the attack was referred to as "D-Day."

Eisenhower was named the supreme commander of this mission, in charge of all the Allied troops. The soldiers loved Eisenhower. He inspired them with his sincerity and easy discipline. He considered the troops' **morale** to be "the greatest single factor in a successful war."

The Allied forces spent two years planning the D-Day invasion. Millions of tons of weapons and equipment had to be shipped to England. More than 1 million men had to gather and prepare for the invasion. Over 2,700 ships, 2,500 **landing craft,** and 700 warships would cross the **English Channel** to put soldiers on the beaches of Normandy, a region in northern France. All of these had to be **amassed** in southern England. Eisenhower was responsible for all the equipment, supplies, and troops that played a role in the invasion.

Another important part of the plan involved deceiving the enemy. The Germans knew there would be an invasion, but they did not know where or when it would happen. The most logical place was at Calais, France. This was the closest point in France to England and meant only a 30-mile (48-km) crossing of the dangerous English Channel.

On the day General Eisenhower was leading the D-Day invasion, his son, John, was graduating from West Point. Later that summer, John arrived in Europe to visit his father. General Eisenhower took him everywhere, including the battlefront. Although John pleaded with his father to let him join a combat unit in France, this was against army rules.

General Eisenhower cared deeply about the morale of his troops. Here he is shown giving words of encouragement to soldiers who were about to take part in the massive D-Day invasion of June 6, 1944.

By filling distant harbors with fake landing craft, the planners were able to trick the Germans into thinking that the invasion would be launched from a **decoy** military base 200 miles (322 km) away from the real invasion.

Shortly after midnight on June 6, 1944, the real D-Day forces left from the shores of southern England about 200 miles (322 km) to the west of the decoy bases. The ships and landing craft traveled 100 miles (161 km) on rough seas. It was a brutal crossing. Some of the troops were lost at sea when their landing craft were swamped. Most of the soldiers were wet, and cold, and violently seasick when they arrived at Normandy. Then they had to stagger into the freezing water carrying heavy packs and make their way onto the beaches with the enemy shooting at them.

Although thousands of Allied soldiers were killed, the Nazis were taken by surprise. By the end of the first day, Allied troops had captured a long stretch of beach. In one day, 132,000 troops and 23,000 **paratroopers** landed in France. Within a month, more than a million Allied soldiers had landed in Europe.

In less than a year, Nazi troops had been pushed back to Germany. They were soon killed or captured by Allied forces. Germany surrendered on May 7, 1945.

Operation Overlord was the largest invasion in the history of the world. Its success was the greatest achievement of Ike's military career. He was hailed as a great hero in the United States, Great Britain, France, and in all the other Allied countries. Later that year, President Harry S. Truman called Eisenhower, now a five-star general, to Washington to become Chief of Staff of the US Army.

When the Germans surrendered in May of 1945, Eisenhower issued the Victory Order of the Day. This stated that instead of celebrating, the troops should remember and honor those who had died. He said this would send comfort to "the loved ones of comrades who could not live to see this day."

As supreme commander of Operation Overlord, General Eisenhower was in charge of the enormous D-Day invasion, shown here. Eisenhower reported the victory, saying, "The Allied force, which invaded Europe on June 6, has utterly defeated the Germans by land, sea, and air."

THE AXIS POWERS

Adolf Hitler (pictured above) was the leader of the Nazi **political party.** In 1933, he became the dictator of Germany, a ruler with complete power over the country. He built up Germany's military. Then he began to take over the surrounding countries. The Germans occupied Austria in 1938, then Czechoslovakia in 1939. When the Nazis invaded Poland in September of 1939, France and Great Britain declared war. The Soviet Union entered the war after Germany invaded it in 1941.

Hitler and the leaders of Italy and Japan had agreed to work together. They called themselves the Axis powers. Japan had invaded China in 1937, but it was not until the Japanese bombed Pearl Harbor in 1941 that the United States became involved in the war. Eisenhower was not involved in the war in Japan, but led the Allies in Europe and Africa.

The full extent of what the Allies were fighting for became clear as Allied forces began to overrun German territory, just before Germany's surrender in May 1945. Liberating troops were horrified to find death camps in which more than six million Jewish people had been worked to death or murdered. Hitler and the Nazis had blamed them for Germany's problems and intended to destroy all Jewish people.

The war with Japan ended after the United States dropped **atomic bombs** on the Japanese cities of Hiroshima and Nagasaki. These acts instantly killed many thousands of people. The Japanese surrendered on August 14, 1945. World War II was over.

CHAPTER THREE

FROM WAR HERO TO PRESIDENT

When the war was over, millions of soldiers were eager to get home to the United States. The families of soldiers started "Bring Daddy Home" clubs to protest that the process was taking too long. Overseas, some of the soldiers were rioting. Even though the fighting was over, the demobilization, or disbanding of the armed forces, was a long and complex task. As the newly appointed chief of staff of the army, Eisenhower tried to speed up the troops' return and to calm the protests at home and abroad.

In early 1948, Eisenhower retired from active duty to become the president of Columbia University in New York City. He also continued to advise the government on military matters.

General Eisenhower waves to a cheering crowd in New York City. After retiring from active duty, he served as president of Columbia University from 1948 to 1950.

One of the problems that appeared after World War II was the rise of **communism.** In communist countries, citizens do not own land and businesses. Everything is owned and run by the government and belongs to the country as a whole. Russia had been a communist country since 1917. In 1922, Russia and the territories under its control became known as the Soviet Union. The Soviet people did not have elections. They also had no personal freedoms, such as freedom of speech or the freedom to practice a religion.

After World War II, The Soviet Union occupied Eastern Europe. It set up communist governments in many countries there and became a powerful empire. This power and the communist ideals of the Soviet Union posed a threat to **democracies.** In response, the United States, Canada, and the nations of Western Europe created the North Atlantic Treaty Organization (NATO). This was a military alliance meant to guard against communist attack.

President Harry Truman asked Eisenhower to go to Europe as the supreme commander of NATO in 1950. His job would be to organize a military force of soldiers from the 11 NATO countries. They would then be prepared to defend Europe against Soviet attack. Even though Eisenhower had retired from active duty, he was still dedicated to his country. "I'm a soldier," he said, "and if you ask me to go, of course, I will go."

In 1948, Eisenhower published a book about World War II called *Crusade in Europe.*

While he was in Europe with NATO, many people from both the Democratic and the Republican political parties urged Eisenhower to run for president of the United States. At first he said he would not run, but finally he agreed to be the Republican Party **candidate.**

President Harry Truman (right) shakes hands with General Eisenhower before Eisenhower departed for France to serve as the commander of NATO forces in Europe.

Upon returning to the United States, Eisenhower chose Richard M. Nixon, a US senator from California, to run for vice president. On November 4, 1952, Eisenhower defeated Adlai Stevenson by more than six million votes.

While Eisenhower was running for president, one of the most important issues had been the Korean War. Korea had divided into two countries: the Peoples Republic of Korea (North Korea), which was communist; and the Republic of Korea (South Korea), which was not. In 1950, North Korea had attacked South Korea. Many people thought this proved that the communists were trying to spread their ideas around the world. The United States and other countries sent troops to help South Korea. China and the Soviet Union sent ground and air forces to support the North Koreans. A bloody war raged between the two sides. Before the election, Eisenhower promised to help end the war as soon as possible.

Six months after Eisenhower was elected, an armistice was signed ending the fighting of the Korean War. Even though the fighting was over, Americans now believed that communist governments were trying to take over the world.

Nearly 55,000 Americans died in the Korean War.

A US senator named Joseph McCarthy used the fear of communism to gain power in politics. He accused many writers, actors, politicians, and other American citizens of being communists. He said they were a threat to the safety of the United States. Many of those he branded as communists had their careers ruined. Americans began to worry that whatever they said against the US government could be used against them. This movement to accuse people of being communist became known as "McCarthyism."

In the 1950s, Senator Joseph McCarthy accused many Americans of supporting communism. Often what he said was wrong or unfair. But at that time, Americans were afraid that the Soviets planned to take over the country. McCarthy fueled these fears and was able to convince people that communism was already a serious threat in the United States.

It went against one of the most basic rights of American citizens: freedom of speech.

Some people criticized Eisenhower for not stopping McCarthy. Senator McCarthy had traveled on Eisenhower's campaign train. Back in 1950, Richard Nixon, who became Eisenhower's vice president, had supported McCarthy's anti-communist movement. He had hoped this would help him get elected to the Senate. But Eisenhower said he didn't want to interfere with Congress. Finally, McCarthy went too far. He began accusing people in the US Army. In 1954, the Senate voted to **censure** Senator McCarthy for his actions.

President Eisenhower did not feel that McCarthyism was necessary to protect the United States. Still, concerns about the spread of communism continued to be a serious issue during his presidency. The struggle between the United States and the Soviet Union became known as the Cold War. Although it never led to large-scale fighting as in a "hot" war, it was a long, hard struggle that cost both countries billions of dollars in defense spending.

The Soviet Union maintained tight control of Eastern Europe and tried to spread communism to other parts of the world, including Southeast Asia and China. At the same time, the United States wanted to establish democracies that would side with the Western countries and be a force against communist aggression.

President Eisenhower liked to have cookouts for friends on the roof of the White House, where he cooked steaks on a charcoal grill.

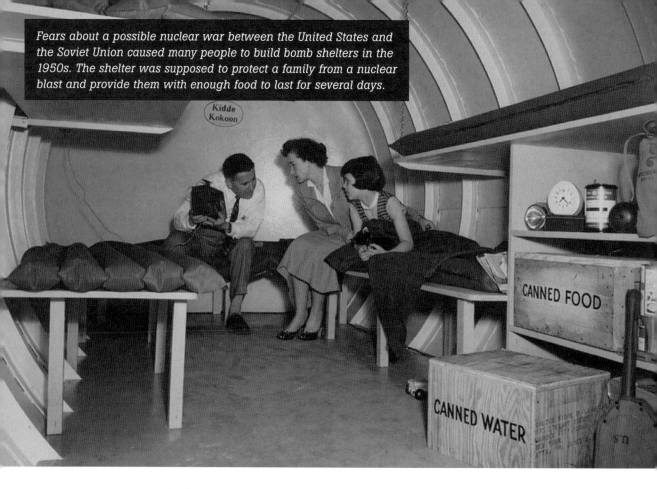

Fears about a possible nuclear war between the United States and the Soviet Union caused many people to build bomb shelters in the 1950s. The shelter was supposed to protect a family from a nuclear blast and provide them with enough food to last for several days.

Both sides supported their positions by developing bigger and more dangerous weapons. This was called the arms race. In 1952, the United States tested its first hydrogen bomb. The H-bomb, as it was called, was even more powerful than the atomic bomb that the United States had dropped on Japan in 1945. The Soviet Union tested its first H-bomb in 1953. Now both sides knew that the other could cause mass destruction in a matter of hours.

In 1955, Eisenhower and Nikita Khrushchev, the Soviet leader, met for talks in Geneva, Switzerland. Both the United States and the Soviet Union had nuclear weapons that were capable of destroying much of the world. The two leaders knew they must avoid war.

Eisenhower suggested that the two nations should allow each other to fly over their military bases. This way, neither country would worry about secret military strength. Khrushchev didn't like this "Open Skies" policy. He said the United States wanted to spy on the Soviet Union.

The fear of a nuclear world war was part of life for United States citizens. Many people dug bomb shelters in their back yards. They kept supplies of food and water in these bomb shelters so that they could live underground if the Soviets fired nuclear missiles at their communities. School children had regular air-raid drills. When a loud alarm sounded, they would practice crouching under their desks with their hands over their heads. For years, people in both countries were afraid that nuclear bombs might one day cause massive destruction and death.

In the middle of trying to stay ahead in the Cold War, Eisenhower suddenly faced a personal struggle. In September of 1955, he had a heart attack while he was on vacation in Denver, Colorado. Members of his staff went to Denver and carried on the president's work. By February of 1956, Eisenhower had recovered. He announced that he planned to run for a second **term.** In November, he again defeated Adlai Stevenson.

During Eisenhower's first term, the minimum wage allowed by law was raised to one dollar an hour.

On June 7, 1955, Eisenhower became the first president to be shown on television in color.

A DECADE OF PROSPERITY

Many middle-class Americans had comfortable lives in the 1950s. In 1954, President Eisenhower urged Congress to pass a **bill** that would allow Americans to pay fewer **taxes.** Businesses could grow larger, and the nation could grow richer. There were more good jobs available than ever before. People had money to spend, and many bought new homes in the suburbs, areas on the outskirts of cities. New houses had been built for the millions of soldiers returning from World War II. They needed new roads, cars, and schools. Building these things created even more jobs. Americans bought electric appliances for their modern kitchens and lawn mowers for their new yards. On television, a recent invention, people watched advertisements for all the things they could buy. Americans went on a spending spree, and manufacturers produced what they wanted. For many, the 1950s were successful years, a time of prosperity.

CHAPTER FOUR

THE SECOND TERM

While Eisenhower was busy with **international** affairs, there were also some serious problems at home. One of these was the struggle for equal rights for African Americans. Although slavery had been abolished for 70 years, most African Americans still lived in poverty. In the South, they were not allowed to live in the same neighborhoods, eat in the same restaurants, or even use the same drinking fountains as white people. There were very few opportunities for good jobs, fair treatment in the courts, or for voting in local or national elections.

In 1954, the Supreme Court had ruled that public schools had to be **integrated.** This meant it was against the law to make African American children go to separate schools. But several years later, most Southern schools were still **segregated.** African American children still were not being allowed to attend white schools. The schools in African American neighborhoods were run-down and overcrowded. They did not have enough books or other supplies.

President Eisenhower and First Lady Mamie Eisenhower are pictured in 1956.

The Civil Rights Movement began during the Eisenhower years. An important event occurred in 1957, when nine African American students tried to integrate an all-white high school in Little Rock, Arkansas. President Eisenhower sent federal troops to make sure the students were able to enter the school peacefully.

On July 16, 1956, President Eisenhower founded the President's Council on Physical Fitness and Sports. This organization has created hundreds of programs designed to emphasize the importance of regular physical activity, fitness, and sports participation for all ages.

As President Eisenhower began his second term, **racial** tension flared in the United States. In September 1957, nine African American students planned to test the Supreme Court ruling by attending an all-white high school in Little Rock, Arkansas. Governor Orval Faubus ordered the Arkansas National Guard to prevent the black students from entering the school.

President Eisenhower demanded that Faubus obey the law and enforce the Supreme Court decision. He said Faubus must allow the students to attend the high school. Eisenhower suggested that the next day the governor should order the same National Guard troops to escort the black students into the school instead of blocking them. But Faubus removed the troops, leaving the young students to face an angry mob of more than a thousand people who were shouting at them and calling them names.

Eight of the African American students were able to enter the school through a side door, but the mayor of Little Rock ordered the police to remove them. To avoid fighting and riots, Eisenhower sent army troops to keep the peace and enforce the law. With hundreds of people watching, the nine African American students walked into the high school on September 25, 1957.

Less than two weeks later, on October 4, 1957, the Russians launched the first man-made satellite into space. It was called *Sputnik*. It circled the Earth every 98 minutes making a continuous beeping sound.

In March of 1957, Congress passed the Eisenhower Doctrine Bill. This law stated that US forces could be sent to nations in the Middle East that were threatened by communist aggression.

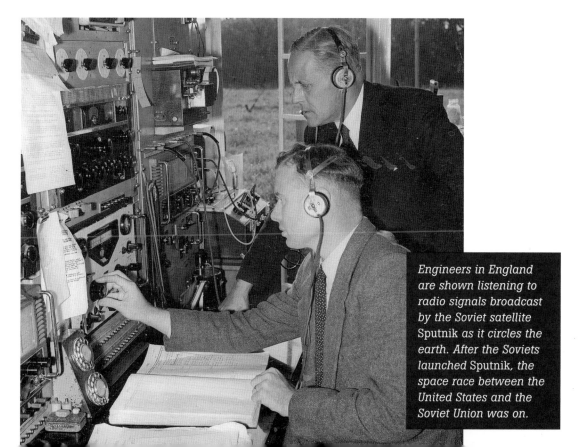

Engineers in England are shown listening to radio signals broadcast by the Soviet satellite Sputnik as it circles the earth. After the Soviets launched Sputnik, the space race between the United States and the Soviet Union was on.

Throughout the United States, people panicked. Since the end of World War II, Americans had believed that their country was the strongest and best educated in the world. Now Russia had demonstrated for all to see that it was the first in space. Americans worried that this could mean that the Soviets were also more advanced in making missiles and nuclear weapons. This seemed like a serious setback in the Cold War.

Eisenhower was not prepared for how much the *Sputnik* launch would damage the self-confidence of the American people. Americans were demanding answers to troubling questions. Why had their country fallen behind? Were schools not teaching enough math and science? How could the United States be secure if the Russians had better technology?

The rise of communist leader Fidel Castro (at left, with arm raised) on the island country of Cuba worried many Americans. Communism was closer to the United States than ever before.

The eight years Ike and Mamie lived in the White House was the longest period the couple had lived in any house up to that time.

Once again the president was under attack from members of Congress. They accused him of not pay-ing enough attention to national security. Eisenhower knew that American scientists were working on a spy satellite, but he could not tell his critics how much he was doing because the projects were classified, or secret. Eisenhower calmly tried to reassure the nation, telling them that he was not the least bit alarmed. Three months later, in January of 1958, the United States launched its first satellite, called the *Explorer*. The space race was underway.

Later, President Eisenhower established the National Aeronautics and Space Administration (NASA) to speed up the space program. He also authorized a billion dollars to improve the teaching of science and math. There was great pressure on him to spend an additional $10 billion on bombers, nuclear weapons, submarines, missiles, and conventional armed forces. Eisenhower refused. He did not want to put so much of the coun-try's resources into defense. He said that the real strength of American democracy came for "the quality of our life, and the vigor of our ideals."

Anti-communism and the Cold War continued. When communist Fidel Castro became the leader of Cuba in 1959, Americans believed it was another sign that the Soviet Union was trying to take over the world. Many were frightened to have a communist country just 90 miles (145 km) away, off the coast of Florida. In 1961, Eisenhower broke off diplomatic relations with Cuba.

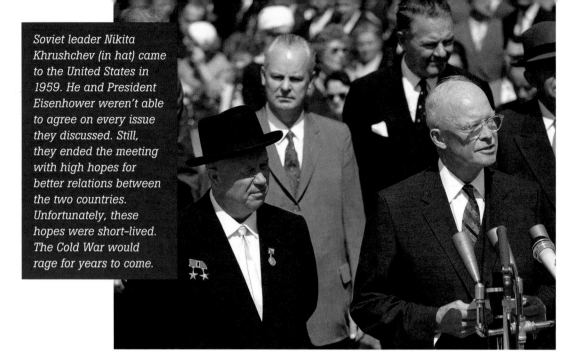

Soviet leader Nikita Khrushchev (in hat) came to the United States in 1959. He and President Eisenhower weren't able to agree on every issue they discussed. Still, they ended the meeting with high hopes for better relations between the two countries. Unfortunately, these hopes were short-lived. The Cold War would rage for years to come.

In hopes of relieving Cold War tensions, Eisenhower invited Nikita Khrushchev to the United States in 1959—and Khrushchev accepted. A great effort was made to make the Soviet leader feel welcome. Although there were some disagreements, the visit ended on a hopeful note. It seemed the relationship between the two countries was improving.

In the spring of 1960, representatives from the United States, the Soviet Union, Great Britain, and France planned to meet in Paris, France. Just two weeks before the meeting, the Soviets shot down an American **reconnaissance** plane over the Soviet Union. Eisenhower admitted that the United States had been sending spy planes to the region for four years, but he did not apologize. He said that if the Soviets had agreed to the Open Skies policy, there would be no need to spy. The Paris meeting fell apart after only two days.

The Cold War was worse than ever. At a United Nations meeting in 1960, the matter of the airplane was discussed. Khrushchev became so angry that he took off his shoe and pounded it on the table.

Eisenhower later said that this decline in relations between the United States and the Soviet Union was the biggest disappointment of his life. His famous ability to bring people together had failed him in dealing with Khrushchev.

In 1959, Alaska and Hawaii became the 49th and 50th states to enter the Union.

At the end of his second term, Eisenhower delivered a televised farewell speech to the American people. He said that the nation was more powerful than ever. It had a huge military force of more than 3.5 million people, and factories that produced large numbers of powerful weapons. The companies that produced these weapons were becoming extremely wealthy from government contracts, and with that wealth came power and influence. He told Americans that the great power of these forces should not be allowed to change the democratic US government.

After Ike's second term ended, he and Mamie retired to their farm in Gettysburg, Pennsylvania. They enjoyed having plenty of time together. "We've always enjoyed each other's company," Mamie once said.

When Eisenhower retired, he had been in public service for 50 years. He had to learn about ordinary life. For example, he didn't know how to use a dial telephone, and he didn't have a driver's license.

In the years following his presidency, Eisenhower remained active and often advised politicians. In this photo from 1969, President Nixon (right) discusses international affairs with Eisenhower. At the time, Eisenhower was recovering from a heart attack at Walter Reed Army Hospital.

On January 20, 1961, Eisenhower passed the presidency to John F. Kennedy. Afterward, Ike and Mamie Eisenhower went to their home in Gettysburg, Pennsylvania. In his retirement, Eisenhower wrote books, painted, and played golf. Politicians continued to seek his advice and support. Years after he left office, he was still one of the most admired men in America.

Dwight Eisenhower died of heart failure in 1969. Today he is remembered as a great general and a popular president. During his 50 years of service to the country, he held positions of great power. But the power itself was not important to him. He wanted to bring people together to accomplish common goals. In so doing, he changed the course of history.

THE CIVIL RIGHTS MOVEMENT

While many Americans had money to spend in the 1950s, about one-fifth of the people in the United States lived in poverty. Many of these citizens were African Americans, who did not have the same opportunities that white Americans had. Although some laws that discriminated against African Americans had been changed, they often were not enforced. During the 1950s, people began to fight this discrimination more than ever before.

In 1954, the Supreme Court ruled that public schools had to be integrated. In 1955, Dr. Martin Luther King Jr. helped organize peaceful demonstrations against discrimination in Montgomery, Alabama. A demonstration is when a group of people with a common goal or belief participate in a march, rally, or other public action to show their support for a cause. Soon there were demonstrations in many parts of the South. For years, white people in the South had tried to keep blacks from voting. In 1957, President Eisenhower signed a law to protect the right to vote for all Americans. Not everyone was happy with these changes. Some people believed that blacks did not deserve equal rights. The photograph above shows an African American student during class in the newly integrated Maury High School in Norfolk, Virginia, in 1959.

The fight for equal rights for all American citizens was called the Civil Rights Movement. Although it gained more attention in the 1960s, its beginnings were in the 1950s, when some Americans were left out of the nation's new prosperity.

1890	**1900**	**1910**	**1920**	**1930**

1890
David Dwight Eisenhower is born on October 14 in Denison, Texas.

1891
Eisenhower moves with his family to Abilene, Kansas.

1909
Eisenhower changes his name to Dwight David.

1911
Eisenhower enters the United States Military Academy at West Point.

1915
Eisenhower graduates from West Point. He is assigned to Fort Sam Houston in Texas.

1916
Eisenhower marries Mamie Geneva Doud on July 1.

1918
The army sends Eisenhower to Camp Colt in Pennsylvania as the commanding officer of the Tank Training Center. He is in charge of 6,000 men.

1919
Eisenhower is ordered to Camp Meade to command a series of heavy tank battalions.

1921
Eisenhower graduates from Tank School at Camp Meade and is placed in command of the 301st Tank battalion.

1922
Eisenhower becomes executive officer for the 20th Infantry Brigade in the Panama Canal Zone under Brigadier General Fox Conner.

1933
Eisenhower becomes an assistant to General Douglas MacArthur, chief of staff of the US Army.

1935
Eisenhower is named senior assistant to General MacArthur, now military advisor to the Philippines.

1936
Germany, Japan, and Italy join forces to form the Axis powers.

1939
Germany takes over Czechoslovakia and invades Poland. World War II begins. Eisenhower returns to the United States from the Philippines.

1940

1941
Japan bombs Pearl Harbor on December 7. Eisenhower is assigned to Washington, DC, as the assistant chief of staff of the War Plans Division.

1942
Eisenhower is appointed commander of European operations and sent to London. He commands the Allied invasion of North Africa on November 8.

1943
Eisenhower directs the invasion of Italy. He is promoted to the rank of brigadier general and then major general. On December 24, he is appointed supreme commander of the Allied Forces.

1944
Eisenhower directs "Operation Overlord," the invasion of France, on June 6. In less than one year, the Allies successfully push the Nazis back to Germany.

1945
Germany surrenders to the Allies on May 7. The United States drops atomic bombs on Japan in August. Japan surrenders and World War II ends. President Truman names Eisenhower chief of staff of the US Army.

1948
Eisenhower resigns as chief of staff. Later that year, he becomes president of Columbia University.

1950

1950
President Truman appoints Eisenhower supreme commander of the North Atlantic Treaty Organization (NATO).

1952
Eisenhower is elected president of the United States. He visits Korea before he takes office.

1953
Eisenhower becomes the 34th president of the United States on January 20.

1955
Eisenhower attends the Geneva Summit Conference in July to meet with the leaders of France, Great Britain, and the Soviet Union. In September, he has a heart attack in Denver, Colorado.

1956
Eisenhower is elected to a second term in November.

1957
In March, the Eisenhower Doctrine Bill is signed. In September, Eisenhower sends US Army troops to Little Rock to uphold a Supreme Court order to integrate public schools. The Russians launch the satellite *Sputnik* in October.

1958
The first US satellite, *Explorer*, is launched in January.

1959
Soviet leader Nikita Khrushchev visits the United States. Alaska and Hawaii become the 49th and 50th states.

1960

1960
A US reconnaissance plane is shot down over Russia. The Paris Summit meeting between NATO countries and the Soviet Union collapses after two days.

1961
Eisenhower breaks diplomatic relations with Cuba. On January 20, he leaves office. He retires with Mamie to their farm in Gettysburg, Pennsylvania.

1969
Eisenhower dies on March 28 at Walter Reed Army Medical Center in Washington, DC. He is 78 years old.

GLOSSARY

allies (AL-lize): Allies are nations that have agreed to help each other by fighting together against a common enemy. During World War II, the countries that fought against the Germans were called the Allies.

amassed (uh-MAST): Amassed means gathered together. A huge amount of military equipment was amassed in England before the invasion of France.

atomic bombs (uh-TOM-ik BAHMZ): Atomic bombs are a type of bomb that causes a very powerful, hot explosion and terrible destruction. The war with Japan ended after the United States dropped atomic bombs.

bill (BILL): A bill is an idea for a new law that is presented to a group of lawmakers. President Eisenhower urged Congress to pass a bill that would allow Americans to pay fewer taxes.

candidate (KAN-duh-dayt): A candidate is a person running in an election. Eisenhower agreed to become a presidential candidate in 1952.

censure (SEN-shur): If the Senate censures a politician, its members state that they think he or she has done something wrong. The Senate censured Joseph McCarthy in 1954.

communism (KOM-yeh-niz-em): Communism is a system of government in which the central government, not the people, hold all the power, and there is no private ownership of property. During the Cold War, a major goal of Soviet leaders was to spread communism throughout the world.

decoy (DEE-koy): A decoy is something used to draw attention away from something else. Before D-Day, the Allies built decoy army bases to make the Germans think the invasion would be in a different place than it really was.

democracies (deh-MOK-ruh-seez): Democracies are nations in which the people control the government by electing their own leaders. The United States is a democracy.

discriminated (diss-KRIM-i-nay-ted): When people are discriminated against, they are treated unfairly because of race, age, gender, or some other difference. When Eisenhower was president, African Americans were still being discriminated against in the United States.

English Channel (ING-lish CHAN-uhl): The English Channel is a narrow strip of water between England and France. The Allies crossed the English Channel and landed on the beaches of France.

integrated (IN-tuh-gray-ted): To integrate is to end the practice of keeping people of different races apart. The Supreme Court ruled that all public schools had to be integrated.

international (in-tur-NASH-uh-nuhl): International means relationships among nations. Eisenhower had to deal with international issues throughout his presidency.

isolationists (eye-suh-LAY-shun-istz): Isolationists believe that their country should not get involved in the affairs of other countries. Some people were isolationists during World War II, and did not think the United States should have anything to do with the war.

landing craft (LAND-ing KRAFT): A landing craft is a type of boat designed to bring troops and equipment close to shore. The landing craft used in the D-Day invasion had flat bottoms so that they could slide into the shallow waters of France.

maneuvers (meh-NOO-verz): Maneuvers are military exercises that soldiers practice to prepare for war. Eisenhower was in charge of training troops and practicing maneuvers.

morale (muh-RAL): Morale is the state of mind of a person or group. Eisenhower thought that good morale was extremely important among soldiers.

Nazi Party (NOT-see PAR-tee): The Nazi Party was a group, led by Adolf Hitler, that ruled Germany from 1933 to 1945. The goal of the Nazi Party was to rid the human race of people the party considered inferior, especially Jews.

occupied (AHK-yeh-pied): An occupied country is one that has been taken over by another country. During World War II, occupied France was controlled by Germany.

Panama Canal (PAN-uh-muh kuh-NAL): The Panama Canal is a waterway built across Panama by the United States. Ships that travel between the Atlantic and Pacific oceans through the Panama Canal save thousands of miles by not having to go around the tip of South America.

paratroopers (PAYR-uh-troo-purz): Paratroopers are soldiers that are dropped from airplanes and parachute into enemy territory. The paratroopers were dropped into France to fight the Germans as the troops were landing on the beaches of Normandy.

political party (puh-LIT-uh-kul PAR-tee): A political party is a group of people who share similar ideas about how to run a government. Germany's Nazi political party came to power in the 1930s.

promoted (pruh-MOH-ted): People who are promoted receive a more important job or position to recognize their good work. Eisenhower was so good at military work that he was promoted many times.

racial (RAY-shul): Racial means having to do with people's races. When African Americans began to demand equal rights, it caused racial tension between blacks and whites in the South.

reconnaissance (ree-KAH-nuh-sentz): Reconnaissance is the inspection or exploration of an area, especially to gather information about military forces. The United States flew reconnaissance missions over the Soviet Union for years during the Cold War.

segregated (SEG-ruh-gay-ted): Segregated means separated by race, class, or ethnic group. The schools in the South remained segregated even after the Supreme Court said it was against the law.

strategies (STRAT-eh-jeez): Strategies are the plans that military leaders have when directing military movements and operations. Eisenhower worked with other military leaders on the strategy to invade Italy in 1943.

taxes (TAK-sez): Taxes are payments citizens make to help support a government. With lower taxes in the 1950s, people had more money to spend on products.

term (TERM): A term is the length of time a politician can keep his or her position by law. A US president's term is four years.

treaty (TREE-tee): A treaty is a formal agreement between two countries stating the terms of peace or trade. After World War I, the Germans signed a treaty that made them take full blame for starting the war.

tuition (too-ISH-un): Tuition is the fee for going to a school. When Eisenhower graduated from high school, he couldn't afford the tuition for college.

THE UNITED STATES GOVERNMENT

The United States government is divided into three equal branches: the executive, the legislative, and the judicial. This division helps prevent abuses of power because each branch has to answer to the other two. No one branch can become too powerful.

EXECUTIVE BRANCH

President
Vice President
Departments

The job of the executive branch is to enforce the laws. It is headed by the president, who serves as the spokesperson for the United States around the world. The president has the power to sign bills into law. He or she also appoints important officials, such as federal judges, who are then confirmed by the US Senate. The president is also the commander in chief of the US military. He or she is assisted by the vice president, who takes over if the president dies or cannot carry out the duties of the office.

The executive branch also includes various departments, each focused on a specific topic. They include the Defense Department, the Justice Department, and the Agriculture Department. The department heads, along with other officials such as the vice president, serve as the president's closest advisers, called the cabinet.

LEGISLATIVE BRANCH

Congress: Senate and the
House of Representatives

The job of the legislative branch is to make the laws. It consists of Congress, which is divided into two parts: the Senate and the House of Representatives. The Senate has 100 members, and the House of Representatives has 435 members. Each state has two senators. The number of representatives a state has varies depending on the state's population.

Besides making laws, Congress also passes budgets and enacts taxes. In addition, it is responsible for declaring war, maintaining the military, and regulating trade with other countries.

JUDICIAL BRANCH

Supreme Court
Courts of Appeals
District Courts

The job of the judicial branch is to interpret the laws. It consists of the nation's federal courts. Trials are held in district courts. During trials, judges must decide what laws mean and how they apply. Courts of appeals review the decisions made in district courts.

The nation's highest court is the Supreme Court. If someone disagrees with a court of appeals ruling, he or she can ask the Supreme Court to review it. The Supreme Court may refuse. The Supreme Court makes sure that decisions and laws do not violate the Constitution.

CHOOSING THE PRESIDENT

It may seem odd, but American voters don't elect the president directly. Instead, the president is chosen using what is called the Electoral College.

Each state gets as many votes in the Electoral College as its combined total of senators and representatives in Congress. For example, Iowa has two senators and four representatives, so it gets six electoral votes. Although the District of Columbia does not have any voting members in Congress, it gets three electoral votes. Usually, the candidate who wins the most votes in any given state receives all of that state's electoral votes.

To become president, a candidate must get more than half of the Electoral College votes. There are a total of 538 votes in the Electoral College, so a candidate needs 270 votes to win. If nobody receives 270 Electoral College votes, the House of Representatives chooses the president.

With the Electoral College system, the person who receives the most votes nationwide does not always receive the most electoral votes. This happened most recently in 2016, when Hillary Clinton received nearly 2.9 million more national votes than Donald J. Trump. Trump became president because he had more Electoral College votes.

THE WHITE HOUSE

The White House is the official home of the president of the United States. It is located at 1600 Pennsylvania Avenue NW in Washington, DC. In 1792, a contest was held to select the architect who would design the president's home. James Hoban won. Construction took eight years.

The first president, George Washington, never lived in the White House. The second president, John Adams, moved into the house in 1800, though the inside was not yet complete. During the War of 1812, British soldiers burned down much of the White House. It was rebuilt several years later.

The White House was changed through the years. Porches were added, and President Theodore Roosevelt added the West Wing. President William Taft changed the shape of the presidential office, making it into the famous Oval Office. While Harry Truman was president, the old house was discovered to be structurally weak. All the walls were reinforced with steel, and the rooms were rebuilt.

Today, the White House has 132 rooms (including 35 bathrooms), 28 fireplaces, and 3 elevators. It takes 570 gallons of paint to cover the outside of the six-story building. The White House provides the president with many ways to relax. It includes a putting green, a jogging track, a swimming pool, a basketball and tennis court, and beautifully landscaped gardens. The White House also has a movie theater, a billiard room, and a one-lane bowling alley.

PRESIDENTIAL PERKS

The job of president of the United States is challenging. It is probably one of the most stressful jobs in the world. Because of this, presidents are paid well, though not nearly as well as the leaders of large corporations. In 2020, the president earned $400,000 a year. Presidents also receive extra benefits that make the demanding job a little more appealing.

★ **Camp David:** In the 1940s, President Franklin D. Roosevelt chose this heavily wooded spot in the mountains of Maryland to be the presidential retreat, where presidents can relax. Even though it is a retreat, world business is conducted there. Most famously, President Jimmy Carter met with Middle Eastern leaders at Camp David in 1978. The result was a peace agreement between Israel and Egypt.

★ *Air Force One:* The president flies on a jet called *Air Force One*. It is a Boeing 747-200B that has been modified to meet the president's needs. *Air Force One* is the size of a large home. It is equipped with a dining room, sleeping quarters, a conference room, and office space. It also has two kitchens that can provide food for up to 100 people.

★ **The Secret Service:** While not the most glamorous of the president's perks, the Secret Service is one of the most important. The Secret Service is a group of highly trained agents who protect the president and the president's family.

★ **The Presidential State Car:** The presidential state car is a customized Cadillac limousine. It has been armored to protect the president in case of attack. Inside the plush car are a foldaway desk, an entertainment center, and a communications console.

★ **The Food:** The White House has five chefs who will make any food the president wants. The White House also has an extensive wine collection and vegetable and fruit gardens.

★ **Retirement:** A former president receives a pension, or retirement pay, of just under $208,000 a year. Former presidents also receive health care coverage and Secret Service protection for the rest of their lives.

FACTS

QUALIFICATIONS

To run for president, a candidate must

- ★ be at least 35 years old
- ★ be a citizen who was born in the United States
- ★ have lived in the United States for 14 years

TERM OF OFFICE

A president's term of office is four years. No president can stay in office for more than two terms.

ELECTION DATE

The presidential election takes place every four years on the first Tuesday after November 1.

INAUGURATION DATE

Presidents are inaugurated on January 20.

OATH OF OFFICE

I do solemnly swear I will faithfully execute the office of the President of the United States and will to the best of my ability preserve, protect, and defend the Constitution of the United States.

WRITE A LETTER TO THE PRESIDENT

One of the best things about being a US citizen is that Americans get to participate in their government. They can speak out if they feel government leaders aren't doing their jobs. They can also praise leaders who are going the extra mile. Do you have something you'd like the president to do? Should the president worry more about the environment and the effects of climate change? Should the government spend more money on our schools? You can write a letter to the president to say how you feel!

> 1600 Pennsylvania Avenue NW
> Washington, DC 20500

You can even write a message to the president at **whitehouse.gov/contact**.

FOR MORE INFORMATION

BOOKS

Herman, Gail, and Jerry Hoare (illustrator). *What Was the Holocaust?* New York, NY: Penguin Workshop, 2018.

Lombardo, Jennifer. *Unsung Heroes: Women of the Civil Rights Movement.* New York, NY: Lucent, 2019.

Marriott, Emma. *Did Anything Good Come Out of World War II?* New York, NY: Rosen, 2016.

Roscoe, Kelly. *Dwight D. Eisenhower.* New York, NY: Britannica Educational, 2017.

Ziff, John. *The Cold War.* Philadelphia, PA: Mason Crest, 2015.

INTERNET SITES

Visit our website for lots of links about
Dwight D. Eisenhower and other US presidents:

childsworld.com/links

Note to Parents, Teachers, and Librarians: We routinely verify our web links to make sure they are safe, active sites. Encourage your readers to check them out!

BIRDHOUSES

Renée Schwarz

302829

KIDS CAN PRESS

To Alex, Sophie and Pippa, my baby birds
And to Dédé, my birdman.

Kids Can Press acknowledges the financial support of the Government of Ontario, through the Ontario Media Development Corporation's Ontario Book Initiative, and the Government of Canada, through the BPIDP, for our publishing activity.

Published in Canada by
Kids Can Press Ltd.
29 Birch Avenue
Toronto, ON M4V 1E2

Published in the U.S. by
Kids Can Press Ltd.
2250 Military Road
Tonawanda, NY 14150

www.kidscanpress.com

Edited by Stacey Roderick
Designed by Karen Powers
Cover photography by Frank Baldassarra

Printed and bound in China

The hardcover edition of this book is smyth sewn casebound.
The paperback edition of this book is limp sewn with a drawn-on cover.

CM 05 0 9 8 7 6 5 4 3 2 1
CM PA 05 0 9 8 7 6 5 4 3 2 1

National Library of Canada Cataloguing in Publication Data

Schwarz, Renée
        Birdhouses / Renée Schwarz.

(Kids can do it)
ISBN 1-55337-549-1 (bound).   ISBN 1-55337-550-5 (pbk.)

1. Birdhouses — Design and construction — Juvenile literature. I. Title. II. Series.

QL676.5.S35 2005   j690'.8927   C2004-901930-9

Kids Can Press is a *l'orus*™ Entertainment company

Contents

More birdhouse information on inside back cover

Introduction

Building birdhouses is a great way to get chickadees, bluebirds, swallows, wrens and many other kinds of birds to nest in your backyard. And with fewer old trees around for birds to nest in, building birdhouses is not only fun, it's important.

The simple woodworking skills you need to make these birdhouses are easy to learn, even if you've never used a hammer or saw. And don't worry if your first houses are a bit lopsided — the birds won't mind!

Most of the houses can be made in an afternoon and will last for years. Be creative and change the designs or sizes, but always make them safe for the birds. Check the chart on the inside back cover of the book for help adapting the projects to different birds.

Building birdhouses is fun, but the best part is when birds nest in them. The sky's the limit!

MATERIALS AND TOOLS

The materials and tools you will need are sold in hardware stores. Also look around your home for extra wooden boards, nails and screws, etc., but always ask first if you can use things.

You will need pencils and rulers to mark and measure materials. Remember to always measure twice so you only have to cut once!

Wood is sold in standard thicknesses and widths that are measured in inches, even though their actual sizes are a bit smaller. For example, if you measured a 1 x 6 board, its real size would be $3/4$ in. x $5 1/2$ in. Common boards are 1 x 2s, 1 x 4s, 1 x 5s, 1 x 6s, 1 x 8s and 1 x 10s. For the projects in this book, buy boards that are the standard thicknesses and widths listed, but cut the exact lengths.

Most of the wood used is 1 inch-thick pine because it is strong, cuts easily and protects the birds from the weather. Exterior grade plywood can be used, too, but nails and screws do not hold as well in the cut edges. Do not use treated wood.

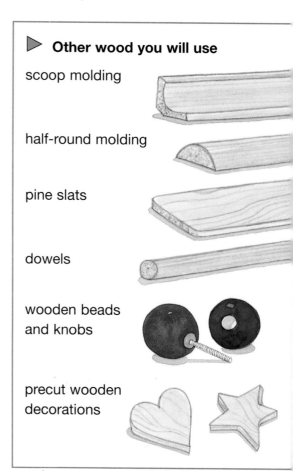

▶ **Other wood you will use**

scoop molding

half-round molding

pine slats

dowels

wooden beads and knobs

precut wooden decorations

4

▷ Some materials you will need for making and decorating the birdhouses

plastic drainage pipes

tin cans

clay and plastic flower pots

plastic funnels

vinyl electrical tape

plastic plumbing T

twigs and branches

exterior latex or acrylic paints

oil pastel crayons, markers, colored pencils

★ *Note: Birds usually prefer plain wooden houses, but if you like, you can decorate your birdhouse with muted colors.*

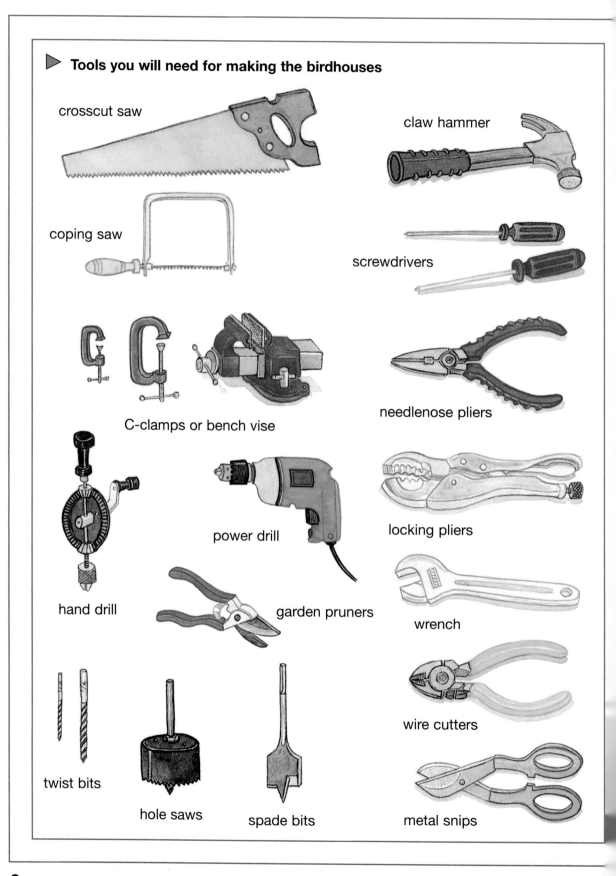

▶ **Tools you will need for making the birdhouses**

crosscut saw

claw hammer

coping saw

screwdrivers

C-clamps or bench vise

needlenose pliers

hand drill

power drill

locking pliers

garden pruners

wrench

twist bits

wire cutters

hole saws

spade bits

metal snips

▶ **For assembling the birdhouses, you will need**

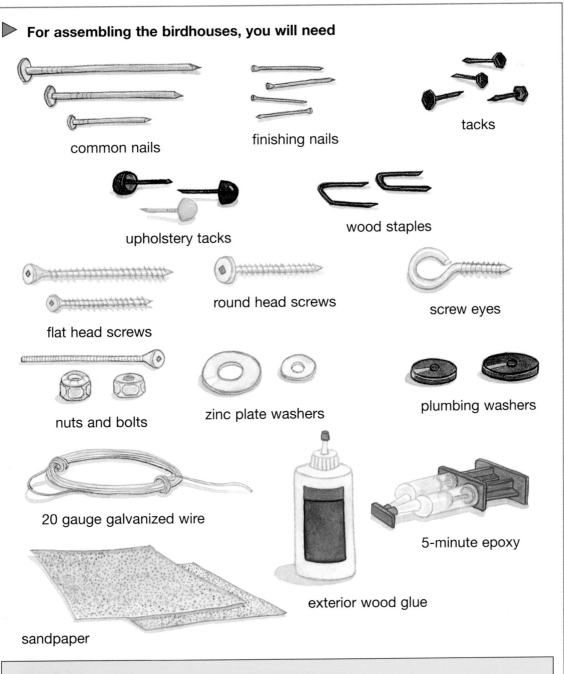

common nails

finishing nails

tacks

upholstery tacks

wood staples

flat head screws

round head screws

screw eyes

nuts and bolts

zinc plate washers

plumbing washers

20 gauge galvanized wire

5-minute epoxy

exterior wood glue

sandpaper

Safety notes:

✱ Follow the manufacturer's instructions carefully when using epoxy.
✱ Always have an adult use the power drill.

✱ Wear gloves and safety glasses when working, because cut metal and wire are very sharp!

Woodworking techniques

Before starting any of the projects in the book, read this section and ask an adult to show you how to use the tools.

Safety

Hand tools are safe when used carefully and properly. Always protect yourself by wearing safety glasses and work gloves, especially when sawing, drilling or cutting. Never force tools, because they can slip and hurt you. Take your time and, if something is too difficult, ask an adult for help. And always ask an adult to use the power drill when it is needed.

Work surface

It is best to use a worktable or workbench. A large wooden board can also be used as your work surface. Keep your work area clean. Sweep up sawdust — it can be slippery!

Clamping

You can use either a C-clamp or a bench vise to hold the wood. It is important to clamp wood to your work surface so it does not move when you are sawing or drilling. The illustrations will show you how to place the wood. Small pieces like branches are difficult to hold in a clamp or vise — you may want to ask a helper to hold them in place.

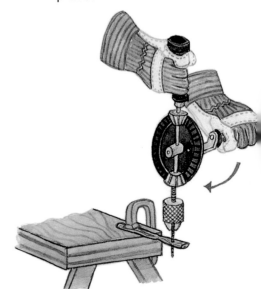

Sawing

Wearing work gloves and safety glasses, clamp the wood to your work surface as shown. Try not to saw, drill or nail through knots in the wood.

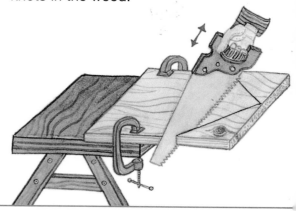

To saw, first pull the saw back slowly a few times to make a notch for the blade. Continue with full strokes. Just let the saw slide — if you push too hard, it will stick or buckle. Try to keep the saw at a 45° angle. Near the end of the cut, hold the part that is not clamped so it does not break off.

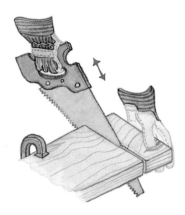

Coping saws cut round shapes and decorative pieces. Draw the shape onto the wood, near the edge. Clamp the board to your work surface and cut the shape out. It is usually easier to make a few cuts that start at different points and meet than to saw the whole piece with one cut. Use sandpaper to smooth rough edges.

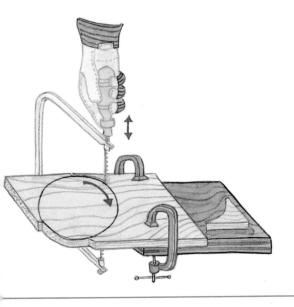

Drilling

Always wear safety glasses and work gloves, and clamp the piece down securely so it does not spin. Have the part of the board being drilled extend past your work surface. Or place a scrap piece of wood underneath first so you don't drill into the table.

Drill bits fit into the chuck, or bit holder, and are held in place by tightening the outer ring of the chuck clockwise (to the right). The size of the hole made depends on the size of the bit used.

Use a hand drill for drilling air, drainage and mounting holes and for drilling pilot holes before nailing or screwing.

Use a power drill with a hole saw or spade bit for drilling entrance holes. Mark the center of the hole and then ask an adult to drill it.

Nailing

Hold the nail in place between your thumb and finger as shown. Tap the head of the nail lightly with the hammer until it stands up in the wood. Remove your fingers and hammer a bit harder. When the nail is well in, hammer with hard strokes. If the nail bends, pull it out with the claw part of the hammer.

Nails should not poke through on the inside of your finished birdhouse! If they do, hammer them flat so there are no sharp points.

Screwing

Screws are stronger than nails but can be easily unscrewed and removed. Choose a screwdriver that fits the slot on the head of the screw. The screwdriver tip should fit tightly so that it does not slip out when turned. Drill small pilot holes first if the wood begins to split. Screws, screw eyes, nuts and bolts always turn clockwise (to the right) to tighten and counterclockwise (to the left) to loosen. Just remember: "lefty-loosey, righty-tighty."

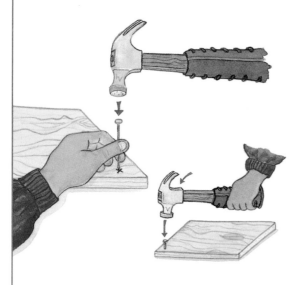

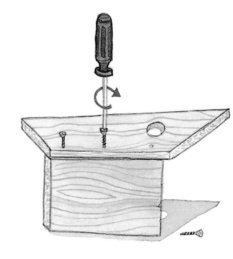

When nailing thin wood slats or branches, drill small pilot holes first so the wood doesn't split.

Tips for mounting and care

Hang your birdhouses on fence posts, in trees or on buildings. Different birds like different spots. Check the chart at the back of the book to see what is best.

● If you have drilled mounting holes in the back of the birdhouse, attach it using screws or wire.

● For houses with no mounting holes, you can screw corner braces or angles to the back corners of the house for mounting it.

● Place the house where there is some shade during the day.

● If possible, face the entrance hole east: birds like the morning sun!

● Place the house where cats can't climb up or jump on it.

● Be sure to make floor drainage holes and air holes.

● Early in the spring, wear gloves to clean out the house by unscrewing the floor. Also check to see if anything needs to be fixed.

● If no birds choose your birdhouse after a year or two, try moving it to another spot.

Robin's delight

For robins, who prefer the open air.

You will need

- two pine boards: 1 x 8 x 15 cm (6 in.)
- thin branches or twigs   • three 2 in. common nails
- about 40 1 in. common nails
- four 1 m (40 in.) lengths of 20 gauge galvanized wire
- small precut wooden hearts   • red oil pastel crayon
- pencil and ruler   • work gloves and safety glasses
- C-clamps, saw, hammer, hand drill with a ¼ in. bit and
  a 1/16 in. bit, garden pruners, wire cutters

1 For the bottom, hammer the three 2 in. nails into one board about 1 cm (½ in.) from the edge of a short side, one in the middle and one near each end. The nails should just poke through the other side.

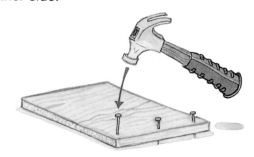

2 Place the two boards together, as shown, and nail them together.

3 Clamp the back board to your work surface. Mark two mounting holes 5 cm (2 in.) from the top. Hand drill ¼ in. holes.

4 Use garden pruners to carefully cut the branches into seventeen 9 cm (3 ½ in.) lengths, three 23 cm (9 in.) lengths and fifteen to twenty 20 cm (8 in.) lengths.

5 So the branches don't split when nailing, hand drill ¹⁄₁₆ in. holes about 1 cm (½ in.) from one end. Clamp the branches to your work surface or have someone hold them while you drill.

6 For the fence, nail the 9 cm (3½ in.) posts about 2 cm (¾ in.) apart (five along the front and six along each side). Nail two 23 cm (9 in.) branches to the back board, as shown.

7 For the roof, nail the 20 cm (8 in.) branches to the top as tightly together as possible.

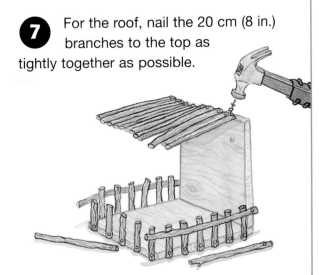

8 Using one strand of wire for each side, wind wire around the posts and crosspieces to hold them together. Also wire a 23 cm (9 in.) branch across the front. Wire the roof branches together near the front.

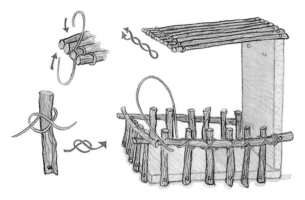

9 Color the wooden hearts and nail them on as decoration.

Moon shelf

For phoebes and other birds who like to sleep under the stars.

You will need

- pine boards: 1 x 6 x 25 cm (10 in.),
  1 x 8 x 14 cm (5½ in.), 1 x 8 x 15 cm (6 in.),
  1 x 8 x 13 cm (5¼ in.)
- two 22 cm (8¾ in.) lengths of ¾ in. half-round molding
- small precut wooden stars and moon
- ten 2 in. common nails • four ¾ in. finishing nails
- exterior wood glue and damp rag
- pencil, ruler, oil pastel crayons
- work gloves and safety glasses
- C-clamps, saw, hammer, hand drill with a ¼ in. bit,
  coping saw

1 For the back, hammer three 2 in. nails into the 25 cm (10 in.) board about 1 cm (½ in.) from the edge of a short side, one in the middle and one near each end. The nails should just poke through the other side.

2 Spread glue on one short edge of the 14 cm (5½ in.) board. Place the boards as shown and nail them together. Wipe off any extra glue.

3 Clamp the back board to your work surface. Mark two mounting holes about 1.5 cm (⅝ in.) from the top. Hand drill ¼ in. holes.

4 Hammer three 2 in. nails along the longer edge of the 15 cm (6 in.) board as in step 1.

5 Spread glue on one long edge of the 13 cm (5¼ in.) board. Nail the roof boards together as shown. Wipe off any extra glue.

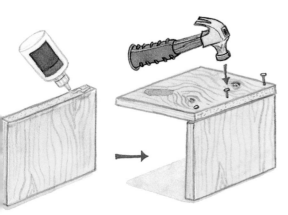

6 Nail the back board to the roof using the 2 in. nails. The peak of the roof should be higher than the back, as shown.

7 Place the molding against the front of the shelf, as shown. Mark the top edge of the roof on the flat side of the molding. Cut along the line with the coping saw.

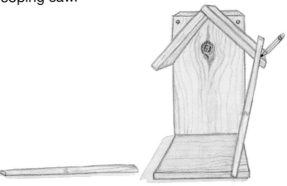

8 Glue the molding in place, wiping off any excess glue. Hammer in the finishing nails, as shown.

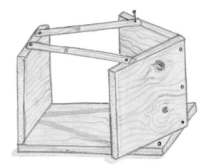

9 Color the stars and moon and glue them on as decorations.

Sunflower pot

A sunny birdhouse to rent to wrens.

You will need

- one glazed or varnished clay flowerpot, about 16 cm (6¼ in.) diameter
- pine boards: 1 x 8 x 17 cm (6¾ in.), 1 x 2 x 40 cm (16 in.), 1 x 2 x 5 cm (2 in.)
- seventeen ⅛ in. pine slats, 1¼ in. x 8 cm (3 in.)
- about forty ¾ in. finishing nails
- sixty to eighty black ¾ in. tacks
- one 2 in. bolt and locknut • one black plumbing washer
- four 1¼ in. screw eyes
- four 10 cm (4 in.) lengths and a 2 m (80 in.) length of 20 gauge galvanized wire
- yellow, light brown, black and green oil pastel crayons
- pencil, ruler, exterior wood glue and damp rag
- work gloves and safety glasses
- C-clamps, hammer, hand drill with a ⁵⁄₁₆ in. bit and a ¹⁄₁₆ in. bit, power drill and 1¼ in. hole saw, coping saw, screwdriver, locking pliers or wrench

16

---

1 Place the pot upside down on the 17 cm (6¾ in.) board. One side should stick out about 2 cm (¾ in.) past the edge of the board. Trace around the pot's edge with a pencil.

2 Remove the pot. Draw a circle about 1 cm (½ in.) outside the first circle, as shown.

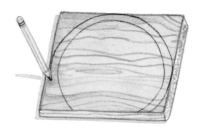

3 Clamp the board to your work surface. Mark an X in the center, 11.5 cm (4½ in.) up from the straight edge. Ask an adult to drill a 1¼ in. entrance hole over the X using the power drill.

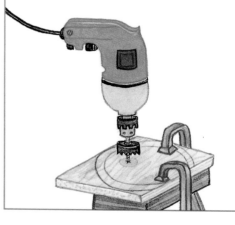

4 Hand drill three 5/16 in. air holes on each side of the entrance hole, as shown.

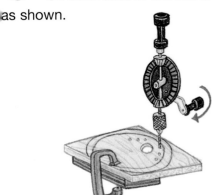

5 Using the coping saw, cut out the circle along the outer line. Don't worry if the circle isn't perfect — its edges will be hidden.

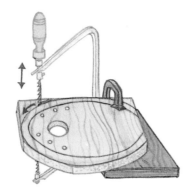

6 For each of the seventeen petals, draw a petal tip onto one end of a pine slat. Clamp the slat and cut the tip out with the coping saw.

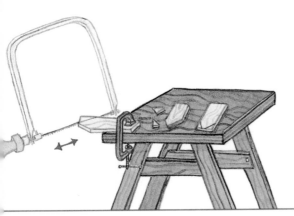

7 Color the petals yellow and light brown roughly and smudge them lightly. Color the center of the flower (inside the circle) black. Color the 40 cm (16 in.) board green for the stem.

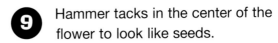

8 Dab some glue on the back of the petals, and nail them around the flower center using two finishing nails for each petal. If the wood splits, hand drill 1/16 in. pilot holes first.

9 Hammer tacks in the center of the flower to look like seeds.

10 Clamp the 40 cm (16 in.) board to your work surface. Mark and hand drill two 5/16 in. holes, one 2.5 cm (1 in.) and another 11 cm (4 1/4 in.) from each end.

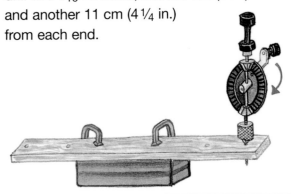

11 Clamp the 5 cm (2 in.) board to your work surface. Mark and hand drill a ⁵⁄₁₆ in. hole in the center.

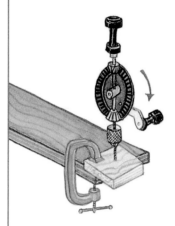

12 Slip the bolt through a hole on the 40 cm (16 in.) board, as shown. Next, slip on the pot, followed by the washer and then the 5 cm (2 in.) board.

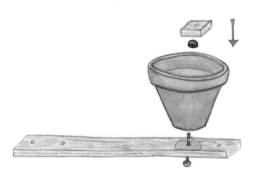

13 Grasping the locknut with the locking pliers or wrench, use the screwdriver to screw the nut onto the bolt. Tighten it gently so the pot doesn't crack.

14 Place the pot upside down on the back of the flower, leaving a gap at the bottom for drainage. Mark four Xs, as shown. Remove the pot and screw in a screw eye at each X.

15 Slip a bent 10 cm (4 in.) length of wire through each screw eye. Twist once to hold.

16 Place the pot between the screw eyes. Wind the 2 m (80 in.) wire around the pot a few times, threading it through the screw eye wires. Twist the ends together, and then twist the screw eye wire ends to hold the pot tightly to the flower.

I love you bird box

Swallows need a little ladder inside so the baby birds can get out.

You will need

- pine boards: 1 x 8 x 23 cm (9 in.),
  1 x 6 x 54 cm (21½ in.), 1 x 8 x 40 cm (16 in.),
  1 x 6 x 14.5 cm (5¾ in.), 1 x 10 x 23 cm (9 in.)
- 23 cm (9 in.) length of 7/16 in. scoop molding
- sixteen 2 in. common nails
- two #6 1½ in. screws • three ¾ in. finishing nails
- #8 tacks for decoration • pencil and ruler
- work gloves and safety glasses
- C-clamps, saw, hammer, hand drill with a 3/32 in. bit
  and a ¼ in. bit, power drill and a 1½ in. hole saw or
  spade bit, screwdriver

1 For the front, mark an X in the center of the 8 x 23 cm (9 in.) board, 17 cm (6¾ in.) from one shorter edge.

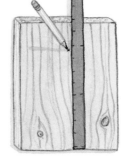

2 Clamp the board to your work surface, and ask an adult to drill a 1½ in. entrance hole over the X using the power drill.

3 To make a ladder for inside the house, saw four grooves below the hole, about 2 cm (¾ in.) apart, as shown.

4 On the 54 cm (21½ in.) board, mark 30 cm (12 in.) on one edge and 23.5 cm (9¼ in.) on the other. Using a ruler, draw a line to join the marks. Clamp the board and saw along the line to make the two sides of the house.

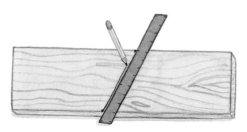

5 For each side, clamp and then hand drill three ¼ in. air holes, about 2.5 cm (1 in.) from the angled edge, as shown.

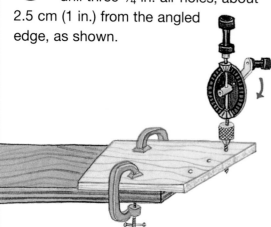

6 For the back, clamp the 40 cm (16 in.) board and mark four mounting holes about 2.5 cm (1 in.) in from the top and bottom corners. Hand drill ¼ in. holes.

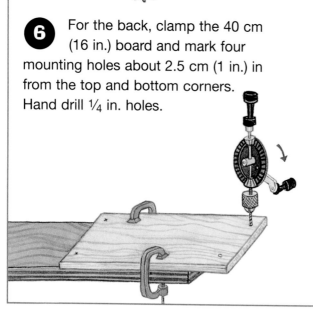

7 Hammer six 2 in. nails into the front board, about 1 cm (½ in.) from each edge, one in the middle and one near each end. The nails should just poke through the other side.

8 Place the front board about 1 cm (½ in.) below the top edges of the side boards, as shown. Nail the boards together.

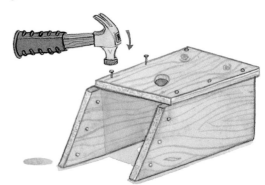

9 Place the back board about 5 cm (2 in.) above the top edges of the side boards, as shown. Nail the boards together.

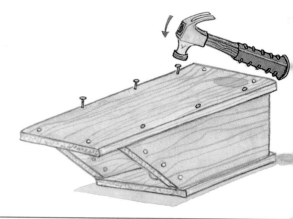

10 Mark and hand drill two ³⁄₃₂ in. pilot holes into the sides near the bottom edge, one about 4 cm (1 ½ in.) from the front on one side and one 4 cm (1 ½ in.) from the back on the other side.

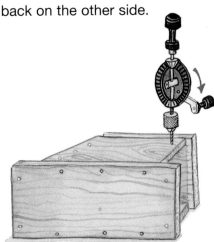

13 For the roof, nail on the 10 x 23 cm (9 in.) board using two 2 in. nails for each side.

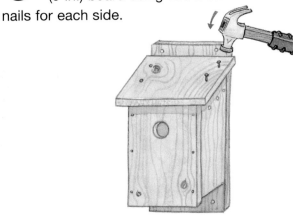

11 For the bottom, clamp the 14.5 cm (5 ¾ in.) board and saw 1 cm (½ in.) triangles off the corners for drainage.

14 Using the ¾ in. finishing nails, nail on the molding to cover the gap where the roof and the back board meet.

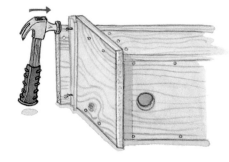

12 Insert the bottom into the house so the base is flat. Screw in the screws.

15 To decorate, nail tacks around the hole. (This also keeps predators from gnawing it to make it bigger.) Draw a heart on the front and nail on more tacks. If the wood splits, first drill tiny pilot holes.

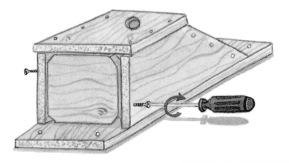

Tree house

A hidden hideaway for a nutty nuthatch.

You will need

- pine boards: two 1 x 6 x 28 cm (11 in.),
  1 x 4 x 19 cm (7 ½ in.), 1 x 4 x 27 cm (10 ¾ in.),
  1 x 4 x 10 cm (4 in.), 1 x 8 x 27 cm (10 ¾ in.)
- sixteen 1 ½ in. common nails • two 1 ½ in. screws
- sixty to eighty 1 in. and 1 ½ in. common nails
- about forty 20–30 cm (8–12 in.) long branches,
  1–2 cm (½–¾ in.) thick
- garden pruners • pencil and ruler
- work gloves and safety glasses
- C-clamps, saw, hammer, hand drill with a ³⁄₃₂ in. bit
  and a ¹⁄₁₆ in. bit, power drill and a 1 ¼ in. hole saw
  or spade bit, screwdriver

1 For the front, mark 20 cm (8 in.) on the edge of a long side of one 28 cm (11 in.) board. Using a ruler, draw a line from the mark across to the corner, as shown.

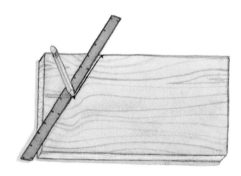

2 Clamp the board to your work surface, and saw along the drawn line.

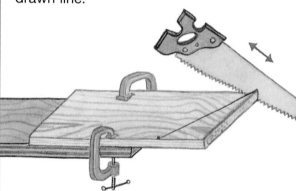

3 For the back, repeat steps 1 and 2 using the other 28 cm (11 in.) board.

4 On the front board, mark an X in the center, 19 cm (7 ½ in.) up from the bottom edge. Clamp the board and ask an adult to drill a 1¼ in. entrance hole over the X using the power drill.

6 Place the front board on the 19 cm (7 ½ in.) and the 4 x 27 cm (10¾ in.) side boards, so the bottom edges are even. Nail the boards together.

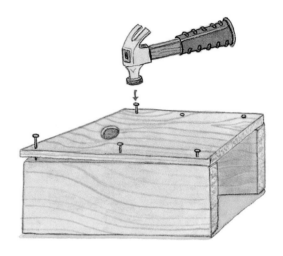

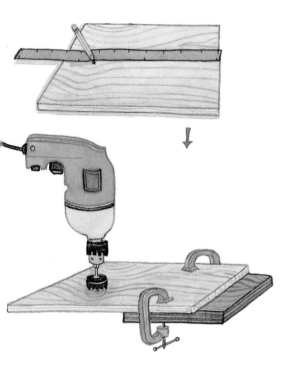

7 Repeat steps 5 and 6 to nail on the back board.

5 Use 1½ in. nails to assemble the house. Hammer three nails into the front board along each side, about 1 cm (½ in.) from the edge, one in the middle and one near each end. The nails should just poke through the other side.

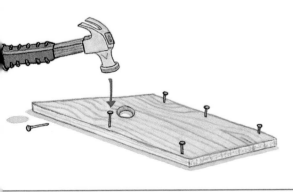

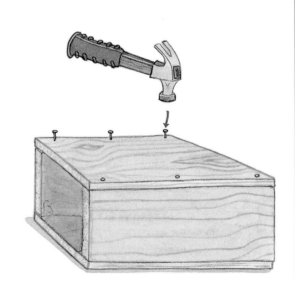

8 For the bottom, clamp the 10 cm (4 in.) board, and saw 1 cm (½ in.) triangles off the corners for drainage.

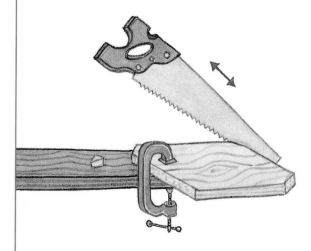

9 Mark and hand drill two ³⁄₃₂ in. pilot holes into the sides near the bottom edges, one about 5 cm (2 in.) from the front on one side and one 5 cm (2 in.) from the back on the other side. Insert the bottom into the house. Screw in the screws.

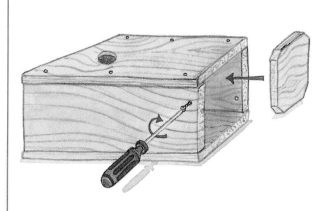

10 For the roof, place the 8 x 27 cm (10 ¾ in.) board on the house so it is even with the back and sticks out about 4 cm (1 ½ in.) past the pointed top. Nail it to the front and back, as shown.

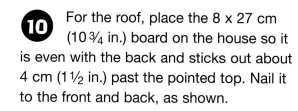

11 To avoid splitting the branches when nailing them to the house, hand drill ¹⁄₁₆ in. pilot holes near the ends.

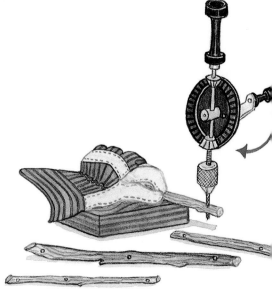

12 Use 1 in. or 1½ in. common nails, depending on the thickness of each branch, to nail the branches to the front, sides and roof, fitting them as tightly together as possible. The nails should not poke through on the inside of the house. Do not cover the screws holding the bottom in place.

13 Nail a few extra branches across the front for decoration.

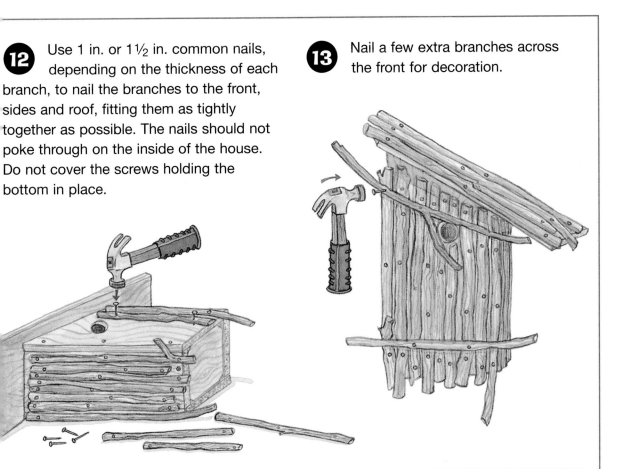

Other ideas

- Cut some branches to make a pattern.
- Use just a few branches.

Crooked little house

Bluebirds will head straight to this crooked little house.

You will need

- weathered or new pine boards:
  three 1 x 6 x 30 cm (12 in.), 1 x 6 x 18 cm (7 in.),
  1 x 4 x 11 cm (4½ in.), 1 x 8 x 28 cm (11 in.),
  1 x 8 x 14 cm (5½ in.), 1 x 2 x 28 cm (11 in.)
- fourteen #6 1½ in. screws • seven 2 in. common nails
- three 1½ in. common nails • four 1 in. finishing nails
- black upholstery tacks • two wood staples
- wood scraps • 6 cm (2½ in.) length of ¼ in. dowel
- red and black oil pastel crayons and black marker
- pencil, ruler, exterior wood glue
- work gloves and safety glasses
- C-clamps, saw, hammer, hand drill with a ¼ in. bit and
  a 3/32 in. bit, power drill and a 1½ in. hole saw,
  screwdriver, sandpaper

1 For the front, mark an X in the center of one 30 cm (12 in.) board, 20 cm (8 in.) from one end.

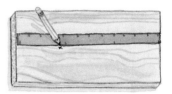

2 Clamp the board to your work surface, and ask an adult to drill a 1½ in. entrance hole over the X using the power drill.

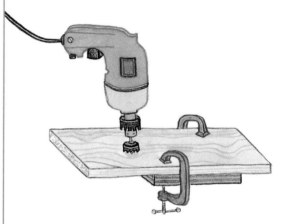

3 On the right edge of the board, make one mark 3 cm (1¼ in.) from the bottom and another mark 9 cm (3½ in.) from the top. Using a ruler, draw lines to join the marks to the opposite corners, as shown.

4 Saw off the triangles.

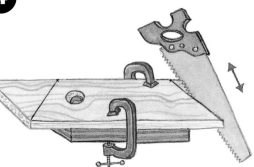

5 Make a mark along the bottom 10 cm (4 in.) from the left edge. Draw a line to join it to the upper right corner, as shown. Saw off the triangle.

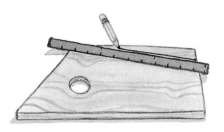

6 For the back, place the front piece on another 30 cm (12 in.) board and trace the cut angles. Clamp the back board and saw along the lines.

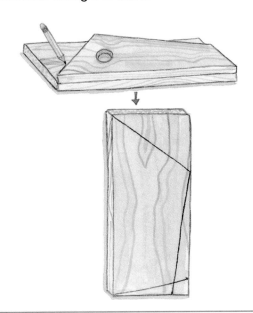

7 For the sides, hand drill three $\frac{3}{32}$ in. pilot holes about 1 cm ($\frac{1}{2}$ in.) from the edge of the 20 cm (8 in.) side of the front board, one in the middle and one near each end. Screw in three screws until they just poke through.

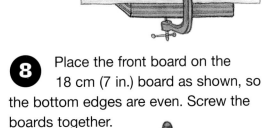

8 Place the front board on the 18 cm (7 in.) board as shown, so the bottom edges are even. Screw the boards together.

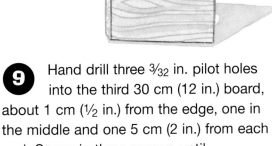

9 Hand drill three $\frac{3}{32}$ in. pilot holes into the third 30 cm (12 in.) board, about 1 cm ($\frac{1}{2}$ in.) from the edge, one in the middle and one 5 cm (2 in.) from each end. Screw in three screws until they just poke through the other side.

10 Place this board against the front board as shown, so the bottom edges are even. Screw the boards together.

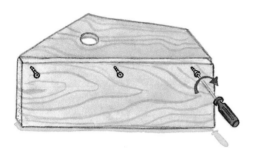

11 Place the back board so the bottom edges are even with the side boards. Hand drill six pilot holes, one in the middle and one near each end of each side. Screw the boards together.

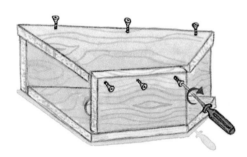

12 For the bottom, clamp the 11 cm (4 ½ in.) board, and saw 1 cm (½ in.) triangles off the corners for drainage. Fit this board into the house so the base is flat. If necessary, cut the bottom smaller to fit. Screw one screw into each side to hold the bottom in place.

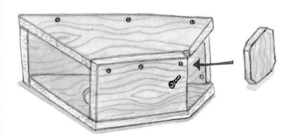

13 For the roof, hammer three 2 in. nails into the 14 cm (5 ½ in.) roof board about 1 cm (½ in.) from the edge of a long side, as shown. The nails should just poke through the other side.

14 Place the 14 cm (5 ½ in.) board on the 8 x 28 cm (11 in.) board as shown, and nail them together.

15 Place the roof on the house so that it is even with the back. Nail the longer roof board to the front and back using two 2 in. nails per side.

16 For the chimney, color the 2 x 28 cm (11 in.) board with the marker and pastels to look like bricks. Hand drill a ¼ in. mounting hole 2.5 cm (1 in.) from one end. Using 1 ½ in. nails, nail the board to the back of the house.

18 Cut the door from a scrap of wood. Color it with red pastel and nail it to the front with finishing nails. Press in a tack for the doorknob. Also nail on a doorstep made from a wood scrap.

17 Nail tacks around the hole. (This also keeps predators from gnawing it to make it bigger.) If the wood splits, drill small pilot holes first.

19 For the mailbox, round off the top of a 2.5 cm (1 in.) square scrap of wood with sandpaper. Hand drill a ¼ in. hole in the bottom and glue in the dowel. Let dry. Color the mailbox, and use the hammer and staples to attach the post to the house.

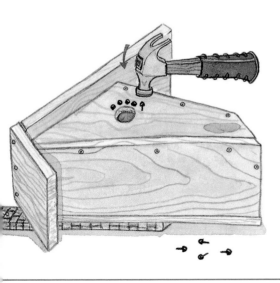

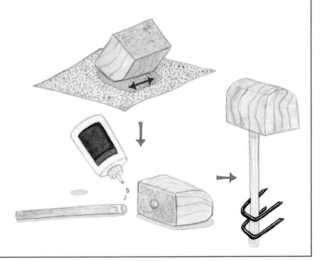

Log cabin

A house sparrow homestead.

You will need

- pine boards: two 1 x 10 x 30 cm (12 in.),
  1 x 10 x 23 cm (9 in.), two 1 x 10 x 29 cm (11½ in.)
- four 2.4 m (8 ft.) lengths of ¾ in. half-round molding
- wood scraps
- eight 1½ in. screws
- nine 2 in. common nails
- four 1 in. common nails
- ¾ in. finishing nails
- pencil, ruler, gray colored pencil
- exterior wood glue and damp rag
- work gloves and safety glasses
- C-clamps, saw, coping saw, hammer, hand drill with a
  ³⁄₃₂ in. bit, power drill with a 1½ in. hole saw,
  screwdriver

1 For the front, mark the middle of the top edge of a 30 cm (12 in.) board. Next, mark 19 cm (7½ in.) from the bottom of both sides. Using a ruler, join these marks to the center mark.

2 Clamp the board to your work surface and saw off the triangles.

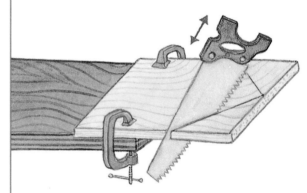

3 For the back, place the front piece on the other 30 cm (12 in.) board and trace the cut angles. Clamp the back board and saw along the lines.

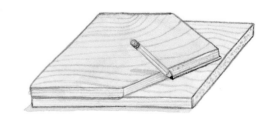

4 For the bottom, clamp the 23 cm (9 in.) board and saw 1 cm (½ in.) triangles off the corners for drainage.

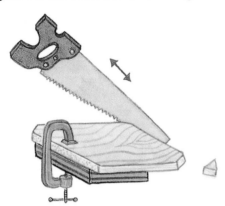

5 Hammer three 2 in. nails into the front board about 1 cm (½ in.) from the bottom edge, one in the middle and one near each end. The nails should just poke through the other side.

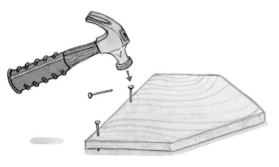

6 Spread glue along one edge of the bottom board. Place the front board on the glued end and nail them together. Wipe off any excess glue.

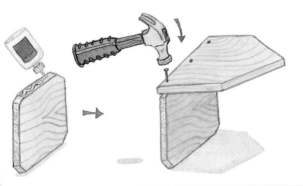

7 Repeat steps 5 and 6 to glue and nail the back to the bottom.

8 Cut eighteen 26.5 cm (10½ in.) lengths of molding with the coping saw.

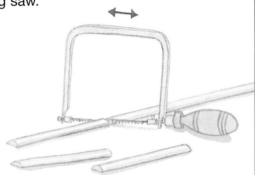

9 Using a finishing nail near each end, nail nine lengths of molding to both sides of the house. Start at the bottom and leave a gap near the edge of the angle for ventilation.

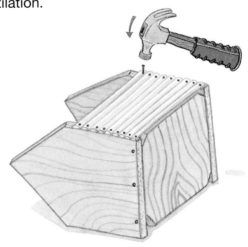

10 Cut a 10 cm x 6 cm (4 in. x 2½ in.) door and a 2.5 cm x 6 cm (1 in. x 2½ in.) doorstep from scrap wood. Glue and nail both to the front with 1 in. nails.

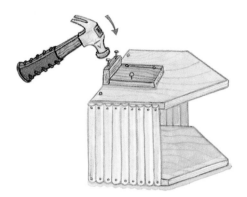

11 Cut a 4 cm x 6 cm (1½ in. x 2½ in.) awning from scrap wood. Spread glue along one long edge and nail it above the door with two finishing nails.

12 For the window, color a small gray square beside the door.

13 For the front, measure and mark each piece of molding you will need, starting at the bottom and working around the door and the window. Saw the molding with the coping saw and nail each piece in place as you go, using a finishing nail near each end.

14 On the front, mark an X in the middle about 17 cm (6¾ in.) from the bottom.

15 Clamp the house, and ask an adult to drill a 1½ in. entrance hole over the X using the power drill.

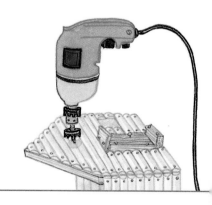

16 For the roof, hammer three 2 in. nails into one 29 cm (11 ½ in.) roof board along the longer side, as shown, until the nails just poke through the other side.

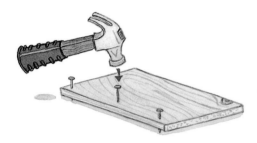

17 Spread glue on the edge of the other 29 cm (11 ½ in.) board. Nail the boards together as shown. Wipe off any excess glue.

18 Measure and mark the molding for the front edge of the roof. Cut with the coping saw and nail in place.

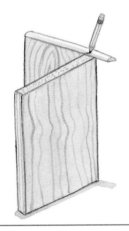

19 Place the roof on the house so it is even with the back. Hand drill four ³⁄₃₂ pilot holes about 1 cm (½ in.) from the back edges, then screw the roof to the back using two 1 ½ in. screws for each side, as shown. Repeat at the front, first measuring how far the roof sticks out.

20 Make a tiny birdhouse from a 2.5 cm x 3.5 cm (1 in. x 1 ⅜ in.) scrap of wood. Carefully saw off two corners to form the peak. Glue and nail on two ⅛ in. thick scraps for the roof. For the entrance hole, hammer in and then remove a 1 in. nail. Glue the birdhouse to the front of the house.

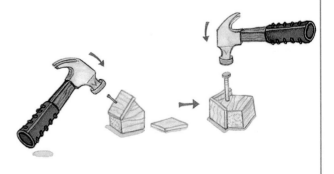

21 Glue tiny scraps of wood across the window to make the panes.

Space condos

A castle in the sky for purple martins, who love to live together.

You will need

- 15 cm (6 in.) diameter lengths of perforated corrugated plastic drainage pipe: 22 cm (8¾ in.), 33 cm (13 in.), 52 cm (20¾ in.)
- pine board: 1 x 8 x 1 m (40 in.)
- exterior plywood: 45 cm x 45 cm (18 in. x 18 in.)
- twenty-four 1¼ in. round head screws
- twenty-four ¼ in. zinc plate washers
- one 20 cm (8 in.) diameter plastic flowerpot
- two 20 cm (8 in.) diameter plastic funnels
- one small wooden drawer or cabinet knob and a nut to fit
- one black plumbing washer
- eight large colored wooden beads
- four 25 cm (10 in.) dowels narrow enough to fit in the beads
- vinyl electrical tape in a few colors
- one 1 in. plastic plumbing T
- nine 1½ in. flat head screws
- exterior paint and paint brush
- white or yellow colored pencil, pencil, ruler, scissors
- exterior wood glue and damp rag
- work gloves and safety glasses
- C-clamps, coping saw, screwdriver, hand drill with a dowel-sized bit, a ⁷⁄₆₄ in. bit and a ³⁄₁₆ in. bit, power drill with a 2¼ in. hole saw

1 For the first tower, clamp the 22 cm (8¾ in.) pipe to your work surface. Use the white or yellow pencil to make a mark 8.5 cm (3¼ in.) from one end. Ask an adult to drill a 2¼ in. entrance hole over the mark using the power drill.

2 Stand the pipe on the board near one end. Trace the inside of the pipe onto the board with a pencil.

3 Clamp the board and cut out the circle with the coping saw.

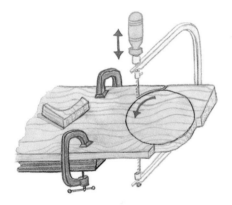

4 Fit the circle into the pipe to make a flat base. Hand drill four $7/64$ in. screw holes around the bottom, through the pipe into the wood.

5 Put a washer on each of four 1 $1/4$ in. round head screws, and screw these into the holes in the base to hold it in place.

6 Hand drill eight $3/16$ in. drainage holes around the pipe, just above the wooden base.

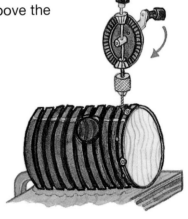

7 Hand drill eight air holes around the pipe about 5 cm (2 in.) from the top edge.

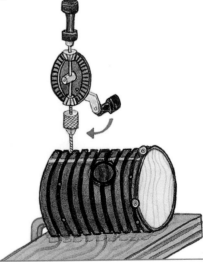

8 Decorate the pipe and the flowerpot roof with electrical tape. Stretch the tape slightly as you stick it on and rub it so it stays on well.

9 For the roof, hand drill a ³⁄₁₆ in. hole in the center of the bottom of the flowerpot. Slide the plumbing washer onto the knob's bolt. Poke the bolt through the hole in the pot and screw on the nut tightly.

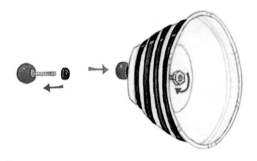

10 Hand drill a hole to fit the dowel on opposite sides of the flowerpot. Place the pot on the pipe and mark the holes. Remove the pot and hand drill holes in the pipe.

11 Put the pot on the pipe and poke a dowel through the holes. Glue a bead on each end of the dowel to hold the roof in place.

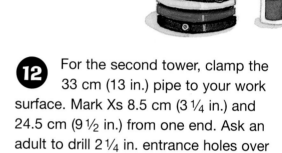

12 For the second tower, clamp the 33 cm (13 in.) pipe to your work surface. Mark Xs 8.5 cm (3 ¼ in.) and 24.5 cm (9 ½ in.) from one end. Ask an adult to drill 2 ¼ in. entrance holes over each X using the power drill.

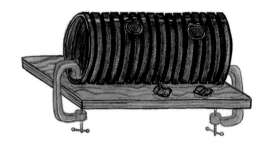

13 Repeat steps 2 and 3 two times to cut out two circles.

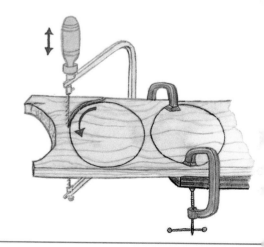

14 Fit a circle into the pipe about 3 cm (1 1/4 in.) below the top hole to make a flat base. Hand drill four 7/64 in. screw holes through the pipe into the wood. Screw in place as in step 5.

18 For the third tower, follow steps 12 to 15, adding a third entrance hole 43 cm (17 in.) from the bottom.

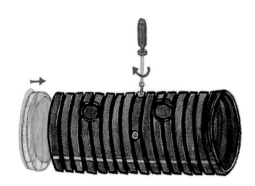

19 For the roof, glue a bead to the end of a dowel and let it dry. Poke the other end through the funnel hole from the inside. Glue a bead on just above the funnel tip to seal the hole. Decorate the tip with an electrical tape flag. Follow steps 10 and 11 to attach the roof.

15 With the same pipe, repeat steps 4 to 7.

16 For the roof, glue the plumbing T to one funnel. Decorate the pipe and the funnel with electrical tape.

20 Ask an adult to cut a plywood base in the shape you want. One at a time, spread glue on the bottom of each house and screw it to the wooden base using the flat head screws. Paint the base with exterior paint and let it dry.

17 Follow steps 10 and 11 to attach the funnel roof to the pipe.

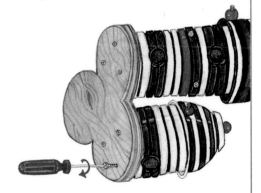

Bird Boot

There was a little chickadee who lived in a boot.

You will need

- an old boot, about 25 cm (10 in.) high
- 10 cm (4 in.) diameter plastic drainage pipe, 20 cm (8 in.) long
- pine boards: 1 x 6 x 20 cm (8 in.), 1 x 8 cm x 8 cm (3 in. x 3 in.)
- four #6 1 in. screws • twelve 1 in. brass nails
- four 1½ in. nails • one black upholstery tack
- two wood staples
- ¼ in. dowel, 6.5 cm (2¾ in.) long • wood scraps
- 1.36 L (48 fl. oz.) empty tin can with the ends removed
- oil pastel crayons and permanent black marker
- 10 cm (4 in.) length of 20 gauge galvanized wire
- exterior wood glue and damp rag, 5-minute epoxy
- pencil, ruler, scissors • work gloves and safety glasses
- C-clamps, coping saw, saw, hammer, hand drill with a ¼ in. bit and a 3⁄32 in. bit, power drill with a 1¼ in. hole saw, screwdriver, metal snips, pliers, sandpaper

1 Clamp the pipe to your work surface. Make a mark 15 cm (6 in.) from one end. Ask an adult to drill a 1¼ in. entrance hole over the mark using the power drill.

2 Stand the pipe on the 20 cm (8 in.) board and trace the inside of the pipe onto the board with a pencil. Repeat to draw a second circle.

3 Clamp the board and cut both circles using a coping saw. They should fit into the pipe.

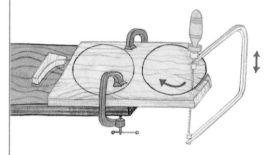

4 Clamp the 8 cm (3 in.) square piece of wood and saw it diagonally across into two triangles.

5 Clamp and then hand drill ¼ in. air holes through one circle and the triangles.

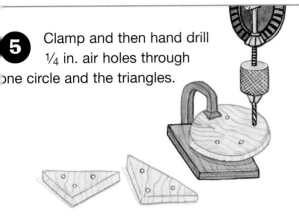

6 Spread glue onto the long edge of one triangle and nail it to the circle with two 1½ in. nails, as shown. Repeat with the other triangle on the opposite side of the circle. Wipe off any excess glue.

7 Insert the other circle into the pipe to make a flat base. Hand drill a ³⁄₃₂ in. screw hole on either side through the pipe into the wood. Screw in 1 in. screws.

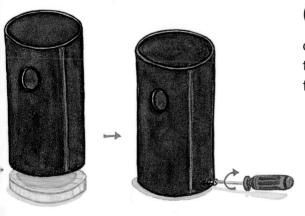

8 Slip the pipe into the boot, base side down. Tie the lace tightly. (Use two laces knotted together to make one very long one.) Feel where the entrance hole in the pipe is, then use scissors to cut out a hole in the boot at the same spot.

9 Insert the top circle into the pipe as shown. hand drill a ³⁄₃₂ in. screw hole on either side of the boot through the pipe. Screw in 1 in. screws to hold the circle in place. (To clean the house, unscrew the screws and remove the circle and roof.)

10 Clamp the boot upside down to your work surface. Hand drill a few ¼ in. holes through the sole and the wooden base for drainage.

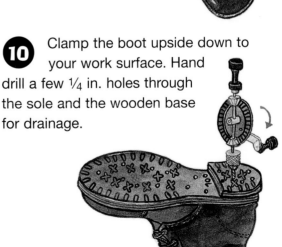

11 For the tin roof, carefully cut the can open, wearing work gloves and using the metal snips. Using pliers, bend and flatten the cut ends twice. Bend the roof in half to make a peak that fits over the wooden triangles. Use the brass nails to nail it to the triangles.

12 Roughly color the roof with oil pastel crayons or permanent markers, or leave it to rust naturally. Color the triangles black.

13 Clamp and cut a door from wood scraps with the coping saw. Press in the upholstery tack for the doorknob. Rough up the boot with sandpaper where the door will be attached. Ask an adult to glue on the door using epoxy. Epoxy a scrap of wood below the door for the doorstep.

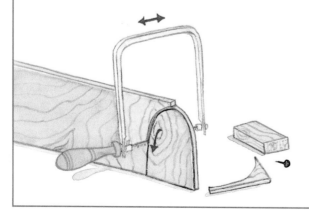

14 To make a mailbox, round off the top of a 2.5 cm (1 in.) square scrap of wood with sandpaper. Drill a small ¼ in. hole in the bottom and glue in the dowel post. Let dry. Color and attach the mailbox post to the sole using the hammer and the wood staples.

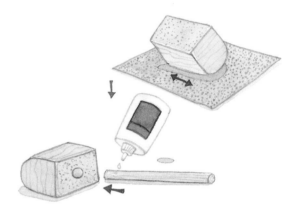

15 Make a sign by hand drilling tiny holes in a scrap of wood. Write the house number in marker on the wood. Slip the wire through a boot eyelet and then through the sign holes. Twist the wire ends together.